Championship Management

An Action Model for High Performance

Championship Management

An Action Model for High Performance

James A. Belohlav

Productivity Press

CAMBRIDGE, MASSACHUSETTS

NORWALK, CONNECTICUT

Productivity Press
P. O. Box 3007
Cambridge, Massachusetts 02140
United States of America
Telephone: (617) 497-5146
Telefax: (617) 868-3524

Cover design by Hannus Design Associates
Typeset by Amick Communications, Newburyport, Massachusetts
Printed and bound by Arcata Graphics/Halliday
Printed in the United States of America

Library of Congress Cataloging-in-Publication Data
Belohlav, James A. (1946–)
    Championship management : an action model for high performance /
by James A. Belohlav.
        Includes bibliographical references and index.
        ISBN 0-915299-76-3 : $29.95
        1. Industrial management — United States — Case studies.
        2. Strategic planning — United States — Case studies.
        3. Organizational effectiveness — Case studies.
HD70.U5B39 1990
658.4 — dc20   90-53062   CIP

The opening quotation for Chapter 1 is from *The Invisible War* by Samuel A. Culbert and John J. McDonough. Copyright © 1980 by Samuel A. Culbert and John J. McDonough. Reprinted by permission of John Wiley & Sons.

The first opening quotation for the Epilogue is from the speech "Productivity Improvement Through Profit Sharing," by Bert L. Metzger. Reprinted by permission of Profit Sharing Research Foundation.

91 92 10 9 8 7 6 5 4 3 2

for Diane, Kate, and Bret

Contents

xi	List of Illustrations
xiii	Foreword
xv	Preface
xvii	Acknowledgments
xix	From the Publisher

CHAPTER ONE • THE SUCCESS FACTOR

4	Good Answers, Bad Solutions
6	Common Themes Create Uncommon Companies
9	A New Corporate Lifestyle
10	Corporate Culture
13	Elements of Style — Correspondence, Alignment, Purpose
17	The Strategic First Step
20	Organizational Commitment

CHAPTER TWO • LESSONS

26	The Dean's List
27	The Actual is Limited; The Possible Is Immense
34	It's the Little Things that Count
39	The Plant Without Jobs
45	Freedom and Respect for the Individual Are the Best Motivators
51	If You Don't Live It, You Don't Believe It
56	Back to the Basics Has Never Been More Basic
62	Meeting the Japanese Challenge
70	Final Comment

CHAPTER THREE • ACTIONS SPEAK LOUDER THAN WORDS

73	Masters of Paradox
75	Principles for High Performance
87	Caveats

CHAPTER FOUR • DEFINING HIGH PERFORMANCE

92 Developing High Performance
102 A Model for High Performance
105 Realities of High Performance

CHAPTER FIVE • FINDING THE YELLOW BRICK ROAD

113 Where It All Begins
118 Generating Confidence
123 One Manager's Story
126 Actions and Reactions

CHAPTER SIX • CREATING YOUR DESTINY

132 Where We Arrive Depends Upon Where We Are Going
137 Fueling the Fire
141 Achieving the Pinnacle
144 You Must Look Backward to Go Forward

CHAPTER SEVEN • SO YOU'RE DOING IT RIGHT, BUT IT'S NOT WORKING

148 Interests and Anxieties
162 Puzzles and Predicaments
165 Solution Through Resolution

CHAPTER EIGHT • TALES TO BE TOLD

170 The Importance of Being Earnest
175 Uncovering Productivity
178 Transformations
182 More and More
183 Not Just Manufacturing but also Service!
186 Some Practical Questions
190 To Be or Not to Be...

CHAPTER NINE • MILESTONES AND MILLSTONES

196   Advantages: Apparent and Otherwise
200   Is a Profit Always Profitable?
203   The Missing 40 Percent
206   The Last Reminder

EPILOGUE

213   Wooden's Wisdom
220   Art Imitating Reality?

221   References
237   About the Author
239   Index

List of Illustrations

Exhibit 2.1   Lincoln Electric's Philosophy
Exhibit 2.2   Lincoln Electric's Merit Rating Form
Exhibit 2.3   H. F. Johnson's 1927 Speech
Exhibit 2.4   "Just Ask" Form
Exhibit 2.5   Position Information
Exhibit 2.6   The Kollmorgen Philosophy
Exhibit 2.7   ServiceMaster's Objectives
Exhibit 2.8   Lands' End Principles of Doing Business
Exhibit 2.9   Customer Letter to Lands' End
Exhibit 2.10   Lands' End Package Insert
Exhibit 2.11   Motorola's Keys to Success
Figure 2.1   Motorola's Participative Management Process
               Principles
Exhibit 2.12   Manufacturing Operations Management
               Development Guide
Exhibit 4.1   "Well, now, what have you two been doing all
               day?"
Figure 4.1   Stages in the Development of High
               Performance
Table 4.1   Ramifications of the Stages of Development
Exhibit 5.1   Memo
Table 6.1   Ownership: What Does It Look Like?
Table 7.1   Functional Silos and Today's Organizations
Figure 7.1   Views of Productivity
Figure 7.2   Potential Problems
Table 8.1   Performance Indicators Used at Clark
               Equipment
Table 8.2   Gainsharing Payout Schedule
Table 8.3   Changes in Experimental Unit
Table 8.4   The Onion Patch Strategy
Table 8.5   DOs and DON'Ts for Stimulating Worker
               Commitment and Quality Performance
Figure 9.1   Strategic Advantages Versus Competitive
               Advantages

Foreword

When I first read Jim Belohlav's book, I liked it. I liked the title, *Championship Management*.

The image of the champion is one with which most of us identify. I have relished those few occasions when I have had the privilege of being a member of a championship team. I took pride in the fact that I had tried to do my part so that together we won.

Championship management conjures the dual role of being the team member — the player — and the leader. Both are vital roles to win in the market.

Business is playing to win ever better. It is heartening to travel throughout America and see the rededication to quality and productivity — championship qualities. This will auger well for the competitiveness of American business. A winning America will create generic wealth. That increment of greater wealth will strengthen our republic.

The work to accomplish these noble objectives will be highly personal, direct, hands-on, participative. Dr. Belohlav integrates these and other leverage factors as a game plan for success.

The game plan in business does not allow for the management to stand on the sidelines like the coach of a sports team; in business, the managers of a championship team are intimately involved.

This book ably addresses the what and the how of players and raises our interest and competence in an inspiring way.

Robert W. Galvin
Chairman of the Executive Committee
Motorola Inc.

Preface

This book is dedicated to the belief that managing and managing for performance are based on two different sets of ideas. The difference is not readily observed either in our general business literature or in our academic textbooks. The process of managing that most of us have become comfortable with looks something like: perception, facts, analysis, action. However, managing for performance also includes acceptance, valuing, understanding, and genuineness as parts of the management process.

The approach of this book is simple. It starts out by recognizing that differences do exist. Management, especially strategic management, is not all the same. What we assume to be good or advanced management may be an illusion. Doing more, or better, is not always the answer either. Next, some companies that are doing it differently are explored. Not that different is necessarily better, but how these companies put the differences to work within their organizations is viewed. Finally, why what these companies are doing ends up creating high performance is examined. More than just understanding the companies presented, this book attempts to explain why some excellent companies become commonplace, why others remain excellent, and why others that appear to be excellent really aren't.

The Japanese companies have forced most of us into at least recognizing that there are differences. The unfortunate part is that we seem to equate performance, quality, and all the other desirable management characteristics with being Japanese. We don't seem to recognize that some American companies are doing just as well as, if not better than, their Japanese counterparts. What is even more unfortunate is that we don't recognize (more appropriate words probably are don't accept) that people within our own organizations are also doing the right things, too! I've seen Fortune 500 American companies looking at other companies that have been branded as being excellent to find out how they do it. This is both good and bad. It is good because it can help management visualize possibilities. However, many of the companies are really looking for panaceas — which is bad. My recommendation is look and listen within your own organization. The answers are probably right there.

Acknowledgments

This book would not have been possible without the help of many people who have unselfishly given their time and energy. I would especially like to thank Dave Drehmer, a friend and colleague, who spent many long hours discussing with me numerous ideas and topics that eventually became the basis for this book. I am also indebted to DePaul University, Br. Leo Ryan, C.S.V., Ken Thompson, and Leon Skan for their assistance in completing this book.

I would also like to acknowledge the following individuals who collectively provided their knowledge and experience to make this book better than it otherwise would have been:

Dave Basseler, Bill Hargreaves, Jerry Willbur, and Ken Fisher of ServiceMaster
Gene Simpson and John Killourie of Motorola
Dick Anderson, Jeff Martin, Suzi Beebe, and Barbara Roberts of Lands' End
Richard Sabo and Keith Cowan of Lincoln Electric
Larry Shearon of Best Foods
Jim May and Roger Mulhollen of S. C. Johnson
Jack Youngblood and Debbie Windoloski of Kollmorgen
Vern Jackson of Auburn Industries
Doug Garrison of Exxon Chemicals
Carl Boyer of Clark Equipment
Ron Brooks of Digital Equipment Corporation
Karl Schaulin and Sally Pearson of Procter & Gamble
John Wooden

In addition, I would like to recognize Betty Harris, Ray Coye, Brad Fox, Gerri Crouse, Scott Stewart, and Lynn Horowitz for helping me in a variety of ways during the course of writing this book.

From the Publisher

We are pleased to publish *Championship Management: An Action Model for High Performance* by James A. Belohlav, professor of management at DePaul University. What makes a high performance company are activities or conditions leading to sustained organizational success. These activities, the author tells us, are: (1) creating recognition; (2) generating confidence; (3) developing fit; (4) providing direction; and (5) building commitment. While these are not topics typically discussed in textbooks, the problems experienced by companies today come from a lack of attention to these aforementioned areas.

Championship Management is written from a managerial perspective within which the author provides an understanding of what a high-performance work system is and how to achieve it. Furthermore, the emphasis is on developing a practical understanding of the process and its application. While many books today contrast Japanese and U.S. business performance, few actually provide a comprehensive, integrative blueprint for action. Jim Belohav does.

Successful companies concentrate much of their attention on creating and maintaining their organizations. In presenting an action model any company can use, *Championship Management* examines the methods of high achievers from a variety of industries: Lincoln Electric's ingenuity, S. C. Johnson's communications methods, Best Foods' reliance on teamwork, Kollmorgen's concern for the individual, ServiceMaster's regard for its people, the Lands' End focus on quality and service, Motorola's Participative Management Process (PMP), and others. The case studies of these companies are inspiring and informative. And although a lot is said these days about the importance of employee involvement and customer service, these are not new concepts. Many company founders themselves instilled such values into their enterprise's daily operations.

In publishing this volume, I wish to acknowledge the efforts of many fine people: David Lennon, production manager, and Beverly Ream, assistant project manager, for producing the book; Cheryl Rosen, series/acquisitions editor, for bringing the book and its author to our attention; Micki Amick of Amick Communications, for her copyediting advice and book composition; cover designer Dick Hannus; and Arcata Graphics/Halliday, for printing and binding.

Lastly, I wish to thank the author for writing this book for us. I admire his respect for and understanding of U.S. companies. Readers will find valuable advice on how to overcome the difficulties facing today's business world.

Norman Bodek
Publisher

CHAPTER ONE

The Success Factor

The Success Factor

Each day we march off to an invisible war. We fight battles we don't know we are in, we seldom understand what we're fighting for, and worst of all, some of our best friends turn out to be the enemy. Our average workday consists of going to the office, sitting in meetings, speaking on the telephone — just talking to people. Yet we limp home physically battered and mentally anguished. It's like being attacked by a neutron bomb — the buildings are intact, but the people are decimated.
Samuel A. Culbert and John J. McDonough

*T*HE idea of being excellent has struck a nerve deep in corporate America. Not because we didn't know about it but precisely because we did. The basis of our past successes seems to have been put aside or forgotten as we searched for new rules. Reality has not matched expectations, though. As a result, seeking the elusive formula for success has become the modern day quest for many current top-level corporate managers as their companies have slipped financially and competitively. The creation of a new and better future has largely remained a dilemma for these companies. The search, however, continues.

Contemporary solutions for declining corporate prosperity have come from many quarters. Academicians and consultants, as well as individuals actually out on the firing line, have presented their own personal remedies for the perceived ailments afflicting corporate America. The cures championed have ranged from zealously exhorting "Japanese-style" management to bringing in the "best and brightest" and going "high tech." Managers, individually and collectively, search the myriad books, seminars, and films for clues to the missing ingredient that will turn things around. All seek something that will transform now languid and sometimes aimless performance into the robust dominance of corporations past.

With bold and sometimes frenzied attempts to chart a new corporate destiny not only for the next decade, but also for the next century, "much of U.S. industry has recently gone on a crash diet to get rid of the flab that caused productivity to lag in the late 1970s. But, as all failed dieters know, there is no faddish or quick way to lose weight permanently. That requires a change of lifestyle." The dieting analogy provides a quite perceptive view of what happens when faddish answers are used at the corporate level.

Good Answers, Bad Solutions

Many contemporary solutions provide, at best, only a quick fix for what is in reality a complex issue. Often the consequence of these solutions is the pointing out of the peripheral and the missing of the significant altogether. Quick and easy answers muddle perceptions rather than create a clearer vision. The various attempts to put the corporate jigsaw puzzle together are futile in the end, because, inevitably, we find more and different missing pieces. The net result is that we have to start all over and try to put the puzzle together again in another, and hopefully better way.

All the quick fix can provide is a veneer of success and a false sense of security. Apparent good fortune can vanish almost overnight with changes in the economic climate, perhaps, never to return again. An unfortunate consequence of the quick fix is that it can misuse or waste precious organizational resources. Of far greater significance, though, it diverts attention away from the *real problem* that needs to be addressed and delays the implementation of the *appropriate solution* for the company.

The illusion of the quick fix is success. The reality of the quick fix is changes that don't substantively change anything — a short-term solution that doesn't make things better, only different. And, most unfortunately, it offers a short-term answer that provides hope for a product that cannot possibly be delivered.

If many contemporary answers turn out to be only a temporary panacea, then what is the right stuff of which successful organizations are made? Is the success factor so elusive that companies may only stumble upon it and may not even realize that they have done so until it is too late?

Solutions to the preceding questions are relatively straightforward. Putting them into action, however, is neither quick nor easy. Many factors create successful organizations. Contemporary business considerations have focused on the importance of being innovative, creating excellence, and developing a customer orientation. These and other essential business objectives, emphasized by Peter Drucker, Tom Peters, Gifford Pinchot III, and others, must *all* be accomplished for a business to attain continuous, long-term prosperity.

Success has many faces. There are many right ways for a business to achieve success. The formula for success is seldom fully attained because it not only varies from industry to industry but from company to company. The sure-fire, blue-ribbon formula for one company probably won't work for another company — at least not very well. There are no shortcuts. Each company must define its own unique path. No one else can.

Common Themes Create Uncommon Companies

In its simplest terms, a business is just coordinated groupings of people doing things to accomplish some common objectives, that is, creating *real* value in the form of goods and services. In attempting to create value, businesses focus on a variety of factors — equipment and machinery, plant location, inventories, market segments, organizational structures, and money management.

There is, however, a common theme within all businesses that are successful and will continue to remain so. These businesses have learned a fundamental truth: *To become a successful business, the business must first learn how to become a successful organization.* Organizations, it should be noted, are people. Just people.

Thus, the prime and overriding concern of the successful organization is how it values and consequently utilizes its people. While readily apparent, this element cannot be overlooked or its value underestimated. The seeming simplicity of this maxim belies its true value to an organization. Utilizing people creates a *strategic* advantage that cannot be matched, at least not easily. This advantage is something that cannot be bought — only earned.

Viewed from a broader perspective, this common theme is, in fact, the precursor to the successful accomplishment of *all* other corporate objectives. For example, one observer has drawn the unmistakable conclusion, "You can't treat your customers any better than you treat each other." Likewise, quality, innovation, or other objectives that we hold dear cannot be accomplished if people in the organization are afraid, ignored, or indifferent.

Utilizing people goes beyond just good management. In practice, good management unfortunately happens to be anything that is currently in vogue. Rather, this theme is a powerful organizational dimension that differentiates being able to do something from being able to do something effectively. What we are concerned with is not what people are doing but how it is being done. Are they actively taking part in the action instead of simply going through the motions? Success comes not from just doing the difficult but, more often, from doing the routine well. Thus, corporate excellence is not so much an organizational objective but rather it is the by-product that occurs while objectives are being accomplished.

Concern for the individual is stressed as a basic cornerstone in many of our most successful American businesses. For example, IBM's fundamental philosophy contains only three simple beliefs. The first of these is commitment to the individual. Put simply and succinctly, "The individual must be respected." At IBM, this commitment serves as the basis for actions within, as well as outside of, the organization and occupies a major portion of management time.

This common theme is also the glue that holds successful Japanese companies together. A penetrating insight into Japanese management is provided by Yoshi Tsurumi when he relates: "Big Japanese corporations treat human resources as their most renewable resources. The hiring, the training, and the promotion of employees and managers are the responsibility of the corporation as a whole. Even a chief executive officer does not dangle the threat, implied or otherwise, of firing a subordinate. Instead, it is management's job to encourage working toward the shared goals of the firm by helping satisfy the human needs of job satisfaction and self-fulfillment."

He continues further by recounting: "One Japanese plant manager who turned an unproductive U.S. factory into a profitable venture in less than three months told me, 'It is simple. You treat American workers as human beings with ordinary human needs and values. They react like human beings.'"

Tom Peters and Bob Waterman, authors of *In Search of Excellence*, amplify the preceding commentary when they note: "There was hardly a more pervasive theme in the excellent companies than *respect for the individual*. The basic belief and assumption were omnipresent. But like so much else we have talked about, it's not any one thing — one assumption, belief, statement, goal, value, system, or program — that makes the theme come to life. What makes it live at these companies is a plethora of structural devices, systems, styles, and values, all reinforcing one another so that the companies are truly unusual in their ability to achieve extraordinary results through ordinary people."

Many companies say that their people are important. However, the excellent companies make sure they carry this view through into their everyday actions. They carefully program their basic values and beliefs into the structure and daily activities of the organization.

In fact, *Business Week* reported, "One *Excellence*-type slogan caught on more widely than any other: 'People are our most important asset.'" I have heard this comment or similar comments on more than a few occasions. A favorite response is, "But where are they on your balance sheet?"

I don't doubt the good intentions of the person making the remark but more often than not it is really only a hollow statement. Sometimes the statement is actually a wish on the part of the person making it. At other times it is just a line, blindly recited because it sounded good when someone else said it. Quite frequently it is just a slogan attached to some grand plan and never gets translated into action. But, slogans come and slogans go. The real test of any belief or principle is, when times are bad, what does the organization do?

The reasons for corporate success in the past will continue to be the same in the future — maximizing the contributions of people. Peak contributions occur when purpose is developed and people are allowed to use their particular abilities. Having success in the past, though, is no guarantee of success in the future. While individual motivation stays relatively constant, the means to satisfy needs changes. The company that stays successful is the one that can continually meld the needs and values of its people within the context of a changing and sometimes turbulent corporate environment. Day-to-day actions that create individual satisfaction are the ones that build commitment and generate high levels of productivity.

A New Corporate Lifestyle

Many businesses today are being confronted by a paradox: As they are getting larger, these companies are actually ending up worse off. Peter Drucker refers to this phenomenon of increasing corporate size coupled with decreasing overall productivity as cancerous organizational growth. While the situation has the appearance of being quite grim, the condition is not as extreme as it appears. As with most basic problems, basic answers provide the only solutions. In this case, the answer for organizations is the same as for individuals — a change in lifestyle. A change in corporate lifestyle can produce significant and sometimes even immediate dividends for everyone in the organization.

The required change in corporate lifestyle must start with a change in perspective. That means viewing the totality rather than simply looking at the parts, viewing the corporation rather than just looking at the individual functions or businesses. In other words, top management must stop taking a short-sighted, micro view when the phenomenon is global. Only when an action is based on an overall corporate system and is an integral part of it will the malfunctioning parts of a business work as they are supposed to.

Equally as important as a change in perspective, a change in thinking must be involved in the new corporate lifestyle. From the top of the organization to the bottom, people will have to begin thinking in ways that may be contrary to their normal inclination and training. Changing this involves using the process of synthesis rather than just blindly applying the tools of analysis as we've grown so accustomed to doing. Analytic tools tend to make us focus on that which can be most easily measured. Thus, our energies get directed to fewer and fewer, but relatively convenient, quantifiable areas. At the same time, we often ignore other less tangible factors — factors that are, in the final measure, more important to long-term corporate health and well-being.

Before the why and the how of this common theme of successful organizations is discussed, we must understand the reasons which cause organizations to operate the way they do — successfully or unsuccessfully. If the names IBM, Procter & Gamble, and 3M are mentioned, certain distinct impressions jump to mind. These impressions generally relate to the perceived basic styles of these organizations. The basic character or style of any organization is what is popularly referred to as its culture. Understanding corporate culture is a necessary part of being successful, but corporate culture is only part of a much broader framework. It provides the foundation for a strong and a successful organization.

Corporate Culture

Corporate culture is a term increasingly used but frequently misunderstood. The term describes an intangible factor that influences virtually every aspect of an organization and its operation. The understanding and application of corporate culture is a hallmark of the successful organization. Suitable cultures that foster success are created and maintained in successful organizations. For our purposes, corporate culture can be defined as:

> _The system of values, beliefs, myths, tools, and practices through_
> _which we respond to the environment. The organizational_
> _culture influences how we get things done. In some cases, it is the_
> _way we get things done.... Regardless of what it says in the_
> _employee handbooks and policy manuals, culture tells people_
> _what is permitted and what is taboo._

Thus, we can see that the corporate culture provides the ground rules for corporate activities, how we interact with others, and perhaps even how we think. Some people act according to these rules and others react without even realizing rules are affecting them. When you wish to know the ground rules of an organization, don't listen to what's being said, but watch the direction the feet move. What people do and how they do it is what's really important.

Thomas J. Watson Jr., former chairman of the board at IBM, describes the importance of culture to corporate success when he asserts: "The basic philosophy, spirit, and drive of an organization have far more to do with its relative achievements than do technological or economic resources, organizational structure, innovation, and timing. All these things weigh heavily in success. But they are, I think, transcended by how strongly people in the organization believe in its basic precepts and how faithfully they carry them out."

IBM's philosophy is further elaborated upon when it was stated: "The only sacred cow in an organization is its principles. No matter what its nature or size, there must be certain bedrock beliefs to serve as a guiding force." The golden ring of success is well within the grasp of any organization, regardless of size — but only if the organization really wants it.

To understand how culture affects an organization's operations, it is important to distinguish between two quite different aspects of corporate culture — its structure and its process. In many organizations, there are basic underlying philosophies or creeds in which the organizations believe and which they use to guide and direct their formal activities. "Progress is our most important product," "The customer is always right," or "Our people are our business" are all mottos representing basic corporate belief systems. The system of basic beliefs provides a foundation or framework for the organization. This philosophy or foundation creates an underlying structure that provides the necessary focal point for corporate activities, both internal and external.

There are, however, day-to-day actions that also define what the corporate culture is. Individuals within the organization use their past experiences, current observations and perceptions, and interpersonal interactions to define the scope of their daily activities. They guide themselves to accomplish corporate as well as personal goals and get through the complicated maze of daily corporate life. These day-to-day activities create the process of a corporate culture.

A lesson that many companies have to learn (and sometimes relearn) is that success is not based so much on how good your objectives are but rather on how well the objectives are carried out. A noted management consultant, Stanley Davis, cogently points out, "If the central beliefs of the culture do not drive the strategy and actions, then the minutiae of daily beliefs will and do." Consequently, if a structure based on corporate values is not operational, then daily actions will create a fragmented structure based on individual or group perceptions and values.

When things start going poorly for a company, who is at fault? Is it the workers? Is it the first-line or middle managers? Is it top management? It's everybody. However, the impetus for change must start at the top. So, the leader's ability to exhibit appropriate behaviors (that is, consistent with the values and goals being expressed) is, perhaps, the most important aspect of a congruent culture. To attain success, a company must carry out this process in a definitive way: "Principles must first be clearly understood by everyone in management. They must be articulated to every employee, repeated so often that everyone understands just how seriously they are to be taken." Just as everyone is responsible when things go poorly, so everyone is responsible when things go well.

An important question for organizational performance: Are what people are doing on a daily basis furthering corporate goals in a manner that is consistent with what the company believes to be necessary for success? Yet, the question is not often asked. Why? Because in many instances, top management is only paying lip service to the corporate philosophy. Instead of walking the talk, they are just talking the talk, giving a new look to the same old ideas and behavior. People learn rather quickly the ropes to skip and the ropes to know. If people at the top show little commitment, why should anyone else?

Elements of Style — Correspondence, Alignment, Purpose

When a company's culture is viewed, several elements make its style or character distinctive. These are: (1) the correspondence of actions within the operating environment, (2) the alignment of interests, and (3) the purpose of the organization. These elements, in fact, ultimately determine whether a strong or weak, pervasive or fragmented, effective or ineffective culture will exist. Overall, these elements influence the balance and the unity of action within an organization.

While all of these elements are concerned with a common end, they mean quite different things in organizational terms. Correspondence of action relates to the coordination of an individual's activities with basic corporate beliefs. Alignment of interests occurs when particular organizational actions have life and meaning for an individual. Organizational purpose provides a reference point and singularity of direction.

Correspondence

Within countless corporate settings, "most issues requiring action are ambiguous, even contradictory, and, with limited information, subordinates rely on their instincts." Inconsistent or poor corporate performance occurs when a correspondence between everyday actions and basic corporate values is achieved poorly or perhaps not at all. People use their instincts to define paths to their individual accomplishments. Personal guidelines are developed to the partial or total exclusion of what the corporate values and goals might dictate. Conversely, successful companies are the organizations that can and do achieve a high degree of congruence between formal corporate beliefs and individual day-to-day behavior.

An effective correspondence results in the company getting the things done that it wants and needs to get done. It means making sure people do the right things and the necessary things so that each individual's actions fit into a cohesive overall framework. The sum of the daily activities equal an intense directional force for all individuals within the organization. This force of action is so powerful that it becomes not just a competitive advantage but an absolute advantage for an organization. This is not to say that people become clones marching in lockstep. Rather, individuals are able to move in a relatively unified manner with little of the intrigue that is associated with many of today's organizations.

Alignment

A second and perhaps more difficult challenge is getting people to want to do the things that the corporation thinks are right. Alignment refers to matching individual and corporate goals as well as developing a harmony of individual and organizational interests. The consequence of effective alignment is a unity of perception as well as a unity of desire. Thus, businesses that understand the dynamics of proper alignment are able to relate daily behavior to the self-interest of the people responsible for carrying out the activities.

Alignment envelops the organization and its members in a kind of web of mutual self-interests. Necessary actions are seen as making sense and being correct from a personal perspective. This means that people want to do the right things. Furthermore, people do what is required because they believe in it. People carry out their activities not because they have to, but because they want to do so.

Purpose

Underlying an effective correspondence and alignment — and consequently the culture of an organization — is its purpose. "Purposes give a company a sense of who it is, where its goals come from, and why trying hard matters. Purposes provide continuity for an organization through its inevitable changes in goals, people, operations, structure, markets and success." Most importantly, a purpose is not getting a 20 percent return on investment or a dominant share of a market. Those are results. A purpose is much broader. It provides a sense of what an organization stands for as an institution.

Why is a corporate purpose important? Perhaps a more significant question is: What is the consequence to an organization when a purpose is lacking? "Having no purpose is exactly as feasible as having no strategy. To have no strategy is to have the strategy of letting the company drift at the whim of external forces, internal politics, and chance. To have no purpose is to have the company stand for nothing."

From a personal perspective, the best an individual can hope for, when no organizational purpose exists, is a job that pays well and perhaps advancement to other "better" jobs. The job becomes the focal point, but the job is essentially meaningless if the organization has no purpose. In the end, just as one job becomes as good as another, so one company becomes as good as another. From an organizational perspective, one action becomes as good as another, which results in conflict and alienation as people pursue their own interests.

While purpose is a nebulous concept to many people, it openly expresses itself in the day-to-day operations of a business. "Virtually every action of a manager or employee is discretionary. A company with clear purposes can expect a higher percentage of discretionary actions to be aligned with the interests of the company." When unexpected situations occur, people can not only take action, but they can take the right action because they understand what is necessary. Conversely, an unclear direction leads to people working solely for their own benefit and trying to satisfy their own interests. Within an operating environment void of purpose, unethical actions can and do take place because the whole is not perceived. Individual actions are seen only in a microcosm. The contrast is sharp and evident. Clear goals and objectives result from a clear purpose, and, in unanticipated situations, good decisions can be made because the direction is unmistakable.

Effective corporate culture provides a synthesis — unifying divergent perceptions with often competing interests into a meaningful whole. Much of our popular literature seems to show that as companies get larger there is a tendency for their culture to fragment. Acquisitions, mergers, or simply getting too big too quickly can all yield an environment that ends up with values that become diffused and a purpose that is confused or even lost. The strategic frame of reference that should be provided by the organization is instead provided for the organization.

The Strategic First Step

When we think of strategic management, we typically think in terms of options and choices for a business. A common prevailing notion is that we simply select among the choices and acquire what we need — much like going to a supermarket. With our acquisitions and mergers, all we are really getting is past history, not the hoped for future. How we fit the organization to its people and how the people fit into the organization is the first and most basic consideration in organizational planning. This strategic decision is not an option. In fact, it is a far-reaching decision that allows the organization to be innovative, customer-oriented, and, in many ways, much more than excellent.

In the competitive corporate world of today, an immediate question of concern seems to be: Why are once successful companies now on the wane? Is it foreign competition? Is it rapidly advancing technology? Those are the pat answers. The real answer is that the weaknesses, which were always there, are now being exposed. The apparent success of the past was only a facade that disguised deficiencies that were already existent. Change has created new business realities.

As companies take comfort in the nostalgia of old triumphs, the vigor and passion generated by past victories has tended to slip slowly away. A sad fact is that many companies today do not recognize the symptoms of deterioration within their own organizations: Daily activities no longer correspond to basic and once widely-held corporate beliefs; people no longer feel any satisfaction from the things that they do in their work; jobs have become nothing more than meaningless sets of activities. Even more tragically, some companies come to the point where they even lose the will to continue. Just as the full effects of cancer don't show up until the very end for an individual, neither do they for an organization.

Why has this happened? Many of our businesses have become preoccupied with techniques and the resultant numbers, rather than with the forces that created the numbers. For a variety of reasons, the numbers have come to be treated as if they are the primary goal rather than the result of the organizational efforts. It should be made clear that I do not believe that using numbers is bad or wrong. In fact, they are quite necessary. The important point is that the numbers that we have come to revere are only an indicator of performance, not an end in themselves. Using the manufacturing arena as an illustration, this exact point is brought out in a comparison of American and Japanese companies. One of the major conclusions pointed out in a research study is that "Americans understand JIT (Just-In-Time inventory method) as techniques, `things to adapt and adopt.' Japanese understand JIT as techniques, but integrated as a way to strengthen people." It is further mentioned that the "Japanese see JIT as a never ending *reform and improvement of themselves*. Improvement is first of the people then *through* the people."

As a consequence of this preoccupation, we view managing today as something that concerns itself more with manipulating numbers than with building an organization. Management, at all levels, has been more concerned with justification than with insight and vision. Donald S. Perkins, former CEO at the Jewel Companies, reflects: "I always thought the way you made a contribution to a company was to build its talent. Now the business world seems to reward good portfolio managers. I feel I'm looking back on Camelot."

Companies that are slipping competitively have lost sight of (or perhaps never even realized) what made them successful in the first place. In spite of everything that has been said or written, most companies don't use their people very well. How people are used is the unique difference between the successful and the not-so-successful organizations and the unique difference between growth and stagnation.

Among companies that do realize their impending plight, more than a few take inadequate measures. In an attempt to shore up lackluster performances, these businesses institute a variety of management development programs designed to make their managers better managers. Indeed, all managers can be better managers, in a technical sense. Successful organizations do not, however, result from individuals simply managing better. We can do all the right things and still not achieve all the right results. Lasting success demands much more from an organization. As Sam Johnson, CEO and chairman of the board at S. C. Johnson Company, so aptly comments, "We don't have to manage for the next quarter, we have to build for the next generation." To build an organization means to build for the future.

What goes into building the right organization? Ken Ohmae, an international management consultant, notes the commonality of critical success factors in organizations: "The most successful large corporations today, regardless of nationality or industry, display a number of common characteristics. They offer job security, tenure-based promotion, and internal development of people instead of global recruiting campaigns. They provide endless opportunities for employee participation. They regard their people as members, not mere employees."

Building an organization means building people into the organization.

Building people into the organization means creating commitment.

Creating commitment means making an environment in which high productivity can become a way of life.

The endgame strategy in all successful businesses is the development of a high-commitment work environment. This is an environment where people throughout the organization not only try to achieve corporate goals and objectives, but also believe in the goals and objectives that they have to carry out. It is a system where the satisfaction of self-interest does not automatically lead to a conflict with corporate goals or goals of other individuals within the organization.

Organizational Commitment

Are high levels of commitment realizable goals or only unattainable dreams for most organizations? One begins to wonder. For example, a report from the Public Agenda Foundation points out a discrepancy in today's American companies that is a major contributor to the current productivity gap. What the study reveals is that there is a growing disparity between the performance of which workers are capable and the performance they are delivering. The research found:

- Nearly one half of the work force (44 percent) says it does not put a great deal of effort into its jobs over and above what is required.
- Fewer than one out of four workers (23 percent) say that they are performing to their full capacity and are being as effective as they are capable of being. The majority say that they could increase their effectiveness significantly.

Why aren't people doing as much as they can while they are at work? Quite obviously, it is because of the environment in which they must accomplish the work. Their responses are revealing:

- Management doesn't know how to motivate the workers. (75 percent agree.)

- All workers get the same raise regardless of how hard they work. (73 percent agree.)
- Today, people want more of a challenge on the job. (67 percent agree.)
- People don't see the end result of their work. (68 percent agree.)

The productivity gap is a real phenomenon experienced on a daily basis. How, then, do we create in our organizations the commitment necessary for high levels of productivity, and what does commitment really mean on a day-to-day basis? One view has been presented by the multitude of discussions on Japanese companies. Is commitment exercising or singing company songs together as popular characterizations seem to make it out? Not really. Commitment is an individual quality. It is not something that exists waiting to be uncovered. It must be actively created. Commitment makes an organization come alive with vitality and even excitement. Promoting their book *Megatrends* in Japan in 1983, John Naisbitt and Patricia Aburdene said: "We were deeply impressed by the commitment of employees. Wherever we went — in taxis, hotels, restaurants, offices, factories — every person seemed to be taking personal responsibility for the success of whatever enterprise he or she was affiliated with." They commented further: "Think about that. Suppose every single person in your organization were taking personal responsibility for the success of the whole organization."

Suppose everyone in *your* company took personal responsibility for the success of the business. Does it sound far-fetched or even impossible? Well, look again. "One of the best kept secrets in America is that people are aching to make a commitment — if they only had the freedom and the environment in which to do so." The findings of the Public Agenda Foundation, indicate that we can do much more than we are currently doing to make our organizations more productive.

Getting commitment involves an evolutionary process within most organizations. The process is a change in lifestyle. It is not creating a new order, but creating new realizations. It is a change, not in content but in form. It is a change, not necessarily in structure, but in style. While the first steps are quite large, they are not impossible. Most importantly, they become smaller the closer we come to reaching our goal.

Success, while easy to recognize, tends to be difficult to achieve and even more difficult to sustain. As we try to imagine what success really is, we have companies that are living, breathing examples of how it can be done. These companies come in all shapes and sizes. We see companies that are new without much excess baggage. We also see companies that have held their competitive ground and prospered in spite of the social turbulence of the 1960s, the rampant double-digit inflation of the 1970s, and the intense domestic and international competition of the 1980s and 1990s. But most of all, we see that not only are high levels of commitment and productivity possible, but many companies are already achieving success — with ordinary people. In the next chapters, we will see how they are accomplishing it.

CHAPTER TWO

Lessons

CHAPTER TWO

―――

Lessons

Wisdom is remembering things everyone else has forgotten.
                                        —Anonymous

W ITHOUT exception, companies that remain successful over time concentrate a significant amount of their attention on creating and maintaining their organizations. They realize that before becoming good competitors they must be good, consistent organizations. In doing so, they create a basic and significant advantage over their competitors and any potential entrants to their industry.

A current tendency is to equate the power of an organization with the financial resources available to it. While access to substantial financial resources can be important, we need to recognize that it only provides temporary advantages that can be overcome rather easily by the next company that has deep pockets. There is another advantage, though, that cannot be duplicated, one on which good, consistent companies rely — the people advantage.

As the keys to success all too often transfer from those with the ideas to those with the MBAs, the reality of management takes on a functional viewpoint rather than an organizational focus. As a consequence, a fragmenting occurs which allows the company involved to become more vulnerable to economic and competitive pressures. Decisions become a series of short-term actions taken in order to make the numbers look good. Emphasis is placed on control rather than accomplishment. That is, trying to maximize what is there rather than trying to create more. Peaks and troughs in productivity and profitability are the inevitable result.

This shift in managerial perspective has taken place in many American companies because of retirements, mergers, or from just plain growing too fast. Mergers and acquisitions inevitably tend to add different cultures; retirements and rapid growth necessitate the sometimes hasty acquisition of people, many of whom will have disparate sets of values. Thus, our most common contemporary corporate activities tend to create a hodgepodge of cultures, philosophies, and values. In the end, this type of activity creates a company with no distinguishing corporate personality at all! Ironically, many of the actions that are taken to reduce risk are, in fact, increasing risk.

The Dean's List

In this chapter, we will present some of the success stories in American business, the corporate Dean's List, and elements of the scripts that have taken the companies to where they are. The companies appearing in this chapter have been subjected to a self-selection process by the toughest group of judges that there is — their corporate peers. The companies presented here are regularly talked to or visited by other companies that seek to learn the secrets of their success.

In other words, these are where other organizations go to school. Not the traditional classroom, but a first class education nevertheless. The group of companies presented in this chapter is not meant to be all inclusive but rather representative. They are large and small, publicly and privately held, and in manufacturing and service industries. Even though each company has its own unique style, each of these companies provides us a glimpse of the future and a sense of the past.

The Actual Is Limited; The Possible Is Immense
Lincoln Electric Company

Lincoln Electric is a nearly century-old company residing in a suburb just outside of Cleveland, Ohio. Lincoln manufactures arc welding equipment and serves the shipbuilding, construction, and oil industries. Lincoln is protected neither by patents nor price supports, and its business is cyclic in nature. In addition, Lincoln has the highest paid workers in the United States. The inevitable conclusion for companies experiencing similar scenarios generally has been one that ended in dissolution, bankruptcy, or being taken over by another company.

The ending for Lincoln's script departs quite radically, though, from the typical rust-belt company. Lincoln has a market share of more than 40 percent and profitability levels that rival or exceed the upper quartile of Fortune 500 companies.

How can such an anomaly exist? A company with the highest paid workers in the United States in a competitive and cyclical industry also has such high levels of profitability? Quite simply, they also have the highest productivity. A research study showed that Lincoln had sales in excess of $167,000 per employee while its industry averaged about $70,000 in sales per employee. (And as a point of further comparison, Mitsubishi had sales of about $110,000 per employee.) Even with such high wages, labor costs amount to less than one-quarter of each dollar of sales.

The Lincoln Solution

What makes management at Lincoln different? Probably the best representation of what Lincoln management means comes by way of example. If we view the year 1982, we see one that was very difficult for a great many companies. Lincoln was no exception. It's sales slipped by one-third creating an excess workforce of more than 10 percent. The response of Lincoln was different than most of its contemporaries. What was the Lincoln solution? True to its motto the company looked past what was actually happening and imagined what could be.

While other companies decreased costs (read that as laying off people) to give the appearance of increased productivity, Lincoln actually increased productivity. The company noticed that a new line of its small welders, which were being handled by independent distributors, had sales of about $1 million. Lincoln took the idled people who made these welding machines and trained them as salespeople to replace the independent distributors. The result was $10 million in sales during the next year. What was the difference? Why was the new Lincoln sales force able to outsell the experienced distributors by a ratio of 10-to-1? Simply, because they were motivated. Their product and their company meant something to them. When they made a call, say, at 3:00 P.M., and the shop operator told them that he was busy and to come back at 7:00 A.M. the next morning, they came back. The consequence was that not only were the shareholders of Lincoln paid their normal return, but the annual bonus averaged $16,000 per person.

The preceding solution is a commonplace event at Lincoln, in good times as well as bad. Lincoln's penchant for productivity creates a curious blend of advanced and what has been perceived by many contemporary companies as outmoded methods. For example, in the early part of the 1900s, Lincoln preceded most other companies by decreasing work hours and providing vacations. Likewise, the much ballyhooed Japanese concept of *kanban*, on-time delivery of inventory, has been a way of life at Lincoln for many years. Yet nearly everyone at

What Is The Lincoln Incentive Management System?
By Richard S. Sabo

We hear a great deal these days about various management systems which purport to give this or that very desirable result. The Lincoln Incentive Management System is really not a system at all. It is a comprehensive philosophy. It is also rules, regulations, practices and programs which have evolved over a 70 year period, growing out of the practical need to control a large dynamic organization.

The philosophy is James F. Lincoln's. He, and his brother, John C., who founded the company in 1895, were sons of a minister, blessed in the case of John C. with an incisive engineering mind and an active imagination; while in the case of J. F. Lincoln, with an equally incisive mind skilled in the arts of motivation, leadership and management of business enterprise. The philosophy is centered in several precepts; 1) people, 2) Christian ethics, 3) principles, 4) simplicity, 5) competition, 6) the customer.

People
They are the company's most valuable asset. They must feel secure, important, challenged, in control of their destiny, confident in their leadership, be responsive to common goals, believe that they are being treated honestly and with integrity, have easy access to authority and open lines of communication in all possible directions.

Christian Ethics
The Sermon on the Mount was the cornerstone of Mr. Lincoln's Christian philosophy. He believed it and he preached it.

Principles
Managers must continuously seek the principle involved in any question or evaluation. A decision based on less than a full awareness of the principle involved will very often lead to an erratic or improper course of action.

Simplicity
Simplicity in thought, policy, principle, buildings, offices, assembly lines, personnel practices and organizational structure all lead to a much easier to manage organization.

Competition
Mr. Lincoln believed very strongly in the universal benefits of competition. Competition is healthy, desirable and as necessary to successful human beings as it is to the successful business.

The Customer
The company exists solely to serve the customer. Our mission is to produce the best possible product to sell at the lowest possible price to an increasing number of customers. If this is successfully accomplished, the needs of the employees and shareholders will be more than adequately satisfied.

Exhibit 2.1   Lincoln Electric's Philosophy   Source: Lincoln Electric Co.

Lincoln in manufacturing is on a piece-rate system, and Lincoln is decidedly not high tech. Instead, the company opts to invest in its people rather than in high-priced machines. Lincoln doesn't go in much for fads. The company examines something thoroughly, and if it increases productivity, it stays until proven otherwise.

Like most of the other companies in this chapter, Lincoln has developed a well-defined point of reference that transcends all corporate decisions. Exhibit 2.1 provides the basis of what Lincoln is all about. Lincoln's current management system is no accident but one that has taken its current shape from methodical change and development that started near the turn of the twentieth century. The Lincoln system of management is put into operation through four basic beliefs. The beliefs that shape management actions at Lincoln are recognition, reward, security, and responsibility.

One of the primary means, recognition, is provided through a management advisory board which has been in place since 1917. Since its inception, the advisory board, currently consisting of 29 individuals, has met with top management every two weeks to discuss matters of mutual interest and concern. This board, while advisory in nature, in fact carries an impact far greater than its name might suggest. Anything is fair game at an advisory board meeting. People have questioned why broken toilets in restrooms haven't been fixed. One time an individual even questioned if the chairman of the board might not be overpaid. What was the response in the latter instance? It was "Maybe I am. Go find out." An answer to an inquiry has to given by the next meeting. If one cannot be given, then a report is given on what was being done.

Probably the most discussed aspect of Lincoln is its compensation and reward system. Employees that are part of the productive process are given a merit rating each year. (See

Exhibit 2.2.) Based on this rating, they are eligible to receive a portion of money set aside by the company. Lincoln has paid this bonus yearly since 1934 (during the Great Depression, no less). The bonus has averaged 95.5 percent of the base wage which is kept on parity with the average wages of the Cleveland area. People earn an annual bonus nearly equal to their earnings for the year! Probably the most novel part of compensation at Lincoln is that the chairman of the board and chief executive officer earn no bonuses or even salary. They receive a percentage of sales as their compensation. That's right. They get paid for what they produce. A refreshing concept, indeed, in a time when we have golden parachutes and top executive salaries that increase as sales and earnings go down. As a last point, I have used the word "earn" when I talk about the Lincoln employees. As Keith Cowan, manager of the Welding Engineering Center, states, "Everyone earns what they get, or they don't get it here." Lincoln's experience has shown that what you pay is not important; it is what you produce. You can pay two or three times the norm, if you can get two or three times the productivity.

Security at Lincoln is a basic and necessary component in its overall system. Thus, a formal guarantee of employment has been in effect since 1958. Employees with two or more years of service are promised at least 30 hours per week. In addition, there is no mandatory retirement. An individual can work as long as he or she is productive.

The last aspect, responsibility, is probably the most important attribute contributing to the continuing success of Lincoln's management system. Responsibility relates to the customer, to fellow employees, and to the company as a whole. Hence, there is no job ownership. Individuals must work where they are assigned, even if it is a lower-paying job or overtime. Further, people are asked to guarantee their work. If a product is

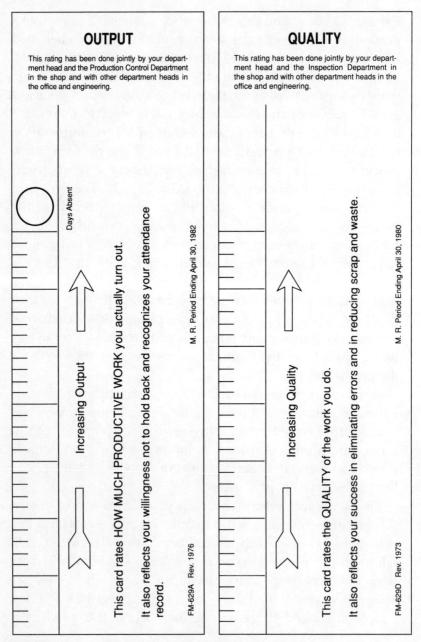

Exhibit 2.2   Lincoln Electric's Merit Rating Form

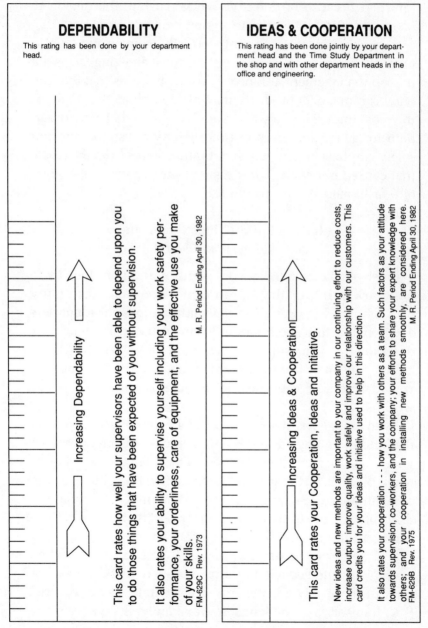

DEPENDABILITY

This rating has been done by your department head.

↑ Increasing Dependability

This card rates how well your supervisors have been able to depend upon you to do those things that have been expected of you without supervision.

It also rates your ability to supervise yourself including your work safety performance, your orderliness, care of equipment, and the effective use you make of your skills.

FM-629C   Rev. 1973

M. R. Period Ending April 30, 1982

IDEAS & COOPERATION

This rating has been done jointly by your department head and the Time Study Department in the shop and with other department heads in the office and engineering.

↑ Increasing Ideas & Cooperation

This card rates your Cooperation, Ideas and Initiative.

New ideas and new methods are important to your company in our continuing effort to reduce costs, increase output, improve quality, work safely and improve our relationship with our customers. This card credits you for your ideas and initiative used to help in this direction.

It also rates your cooperation - - - how you work with others as a team. Such factors as your attitude towards supervision, co-workers, and the company; your efforts to share your expert knowledge with others; and your cooperation in installing new methods smoothly, are considered here.

FM-629B   Rev. 1975

M. R. Period Ending April 30, 1982

Source: Lincoln Electric Co.

returned because of defective workmanship, the person responsible repairs the product at that person's own cost.

Arguably, Lincoln is the most productive company in America today, perhaps, in the world. But the most amazing fact is that the top management at Lincoln Electric believes that the company can make its productivity considerably better. Perhaps, the most important message from Lincoln is that the primary path to lasting increases in productivity doesn't come from solely emphasizing high tech but rather stems from the reason that caused our country to prosper in the first place — good, old-fashioned Yankee ingenuity.

It's the Little Things that Count
S. C. Johnson and Son, Inc.

Most people recognize S. C. Johnson and Son, Inc., by its hallmark product line — Johnson Wax. As a company, S. C. Johnson is as imposing as its international headquarters, a national historic landmark in Racine, Wisconsin, which was designed by the master architect Frank Lloyd Wright. This $2 billion consumer products giant is made up of 46 companies spread across 45 countries. It employs about 11,000 people worldwide.

Even though it is quite large, S. C. Johnson never evolved into the kind of entangled morass of people that is literally strangling many of its contemporaries. In fact, just the opposite has taken place: S. C. Johnson has been named one of the 100 best companies to work for in America. What magic formula does S. C. Johnson use to create an environment that allows both the company and its people to prosper?

S. C. Johnson can be described as a classless society where everyone is allowed to take part in the success of the organization. But probably a better or more accurate way to describe S. C. Johnson is as the Johnson Wax family. Even after retirement, one always remains part of the Johnson clan. Today's spirit of S. C. Johnson was a belief of several generations, however, as Exhibit 2.3 testifies.

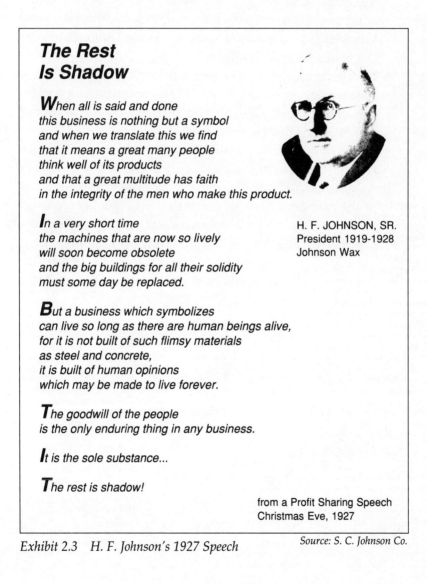

The Rest Is Shadow

When all is said and done
this business is nothing but a symbol
and when we translate this we find
that it means a great many people
think well of its products
and that a great multitude has faith
in the integrity of the men who make this product.

In a very short time
the machines that are now so lively
will soon become obsolete
and the big buildings for all their solidity
must some day be replaced.

But a business which symbolizes
can live so long as there are human beings alive,
for it is not built of such flimsy materials
as steel and concrete,
it is built of human opinions
which may be made to live forever.

The goodwill of the people
is the only enduring thing in any business.

It is the sole substance...

The rest is shadow!

H. F. JOHNSON, SR.
President 1919-1928
Johnson Wax

from a Profit Sharing Speech
Christmas Eve, 1927

Exhibit 2.3   H. F. Johnson's 1927 Speech   Source: S. C. Johnson Co.

Several recent incidents typify everyday life at S. C. Johnson:

- Morale was low at the operations in Great Britain when the employees didn't see how they fit in as part of the company. The cure? Five hundred British employees were brought in for one week to see the United States and visit the company headquarters.
- In the company fitness center, it is commonplace to see employees from every level of the company taking part together in recreational activities and playing on intramural sports teams during their off-hours.
- As one talks to Roger Mulhollen, retired vice-president of corporate personnel, about S. C. Johnson, he will recount how, in his first days with the corporation, he went to eat at the cafeteria. At a company that previously employed him, there were several cafeterias each serving a different segment of the employee population (workers, managers, etc.). The amazing sight for Roger was that everyone ate together at S. C. Johnson. That first day he shared his lunch with a vice-president and an R&D technician.

An often heard axiom is, "Take care of the little things and the big things will take care of themselves." S. C. Johnson takes this old saw to heart. It is a big company that prides itself on taking care of the little things.

The small things are woven throughout the fabric of the organization. We see, for example, at the "company store" employees can purchase Johnson products at cost and sometimes even receive certain products for free. We see a profit-sharing plan was instituted over seventy years ago. And currently, we see S. C. Johnson creating a daycare program to take care of another of the needs of its Johnson Wax family. The list could go on and on. What we see is that the magic formula is really just a simple formula. A simple formula that is pursued relentlessly on the part of the company.

Perhaps, the heart of the success is a built-in process that continually demonstrates the company's concern. It is a program of communication and information that is at the same time formal and informal, written and oral, regular and as needed. But what does this mean? Almost any company will tell you that it strives for better communication among employees, and some companies will even show you their programs. S. C. Johnson goes past just communication. Three examples illustrate the effort the S. C. Johnson has expended: the Just Ask program, the Johnson Wax Weekly, and the employees communications meetings. These separate but interrelated programs not only provide a network, but also provide a safety net to ensure everyone is heard and participates.

The Just Ask program allows any person within the company to ask confidentially any question of concern. (See Exhibit 2.4.) Individuals receive a prompt, personal reply to their inquiries at their homes. Items of general interest are reproduced in the Johnson Wax Weekly, unless the writer of the inquiry requests otherwise. In addition, all of the Just Ask inquiries and replies are sent to the managers each month.

The Johnson Wax Weekly is an in-house newspaper that has reported on the significant and insignificant, global and local, and corporate and individual activities since 1958. It is a potpourri of information, events, and activities. Above all, though, it is the newspaper of and for the Johnson Wax family. A typical issue reports on corporate activities such as a business unit or new products, lists classified advertisements, provides extensive recreational information, presents Just Ask questions and answers, and ends by spotlighting some employees of the Johnson Wax family.

Just as many companies have stockholders meetings,

Johnson Wax

Just Ask?

"Just Ask" is a communications channel to provide employees with answers to complaints, questions and opinions concerning our company. Letters should be submitted to the Just Ask Coordinator on this pre-addressed, postage-paid form. Replies to signed letters are mailed to the home; those of general interest are selected for publication in the Johnson Wax Weekly unless the writer requests otherwise. **All** replies are distributed to managers each month.

All writers are encouraged to sign their letters so the Just Ask Coordinator can contact them in case a question needs clarification. Unsigned letters can be answered only if they are suitable for publication. **Names are treated in strictest confidence**. Only the Just Ask Coordinator will see your name.

Only one person should sign this form. Please use separate form for each subject.

Date _____

_____

_____

_____

_____

If additional space is required, use a separate piece of paper and enclose in this form.

DO NOT WRITE HERE

● ●

This Portion is Kept Confidential by the Just Ask Coordinator.

Check_____ if you do not want your letter published in the <u>Johnson Wax Weekly</u>.

Check_____ if, instead of a mailed reply, you prefer to discuss this matter with a qualified person. (The Just Ask Coordinator will arrange a meeting.)

Please Print

Name _____

Home Address _____

City _____ State _____ Zip Code _____

Station Number _____ Position/Title _____

Exhibit 2.4   *"Just Ask" Form*

Source: S. C. Johnson Co.

S. C. Johnson has meetings for its employees. At these meetings, top management reports on the state of the company and answers questions from the employees. The reports are given several times during the span of a week so that everyone can attend. Even the forgotten groups in most companies, the second and third shifts, get to meet with someone from Johnson Wax. When I say someone from Johnson Wax, I mean someone named Johnson. When employee communications meetings are held, Sam Johnson, chairman of the board, makes a point to appear before these employees.

What makes S. C. Johnson unique? The little things. The things that are normally forgotten in the rush of big business are not forgotten at S. C. Johnson. Because of that, as busy as everyone is, there is always time for a smile.

The Plant Without Jobs
Best Foods Company

Which of the following is the most difficult organization to join?

(a) University of Chicago MBA program
(b) Harvard University MBA program
(c) Stanford University MBA program
(d) Best Foods plant, Little Rock, Arkansas

If you answered (d), you were correct. Recently, this food processing plant decided it needed six more employees. When the employment notice went out, 5,228 individuals lined up outside the plant to apply for the six positions. While the applicants were waiting, it started to rain. Soon the rain started to come down rather heavily. Something very interesting happened then. Nobody left! All the people remained standing in a heavy downpour in order to get their chance to work at this plant. This incident testifies to the quality of the working environment at this Best Foods plant. With the human resource manager acting as a resource, the six people were eventually selected and hired by an ad hoc worker committee.

What would create such a high demand for a job in this particular plant? We can see from the application in Exhibit 2.5 that no glamorous positions existed, only a second shift job that required working on the weekends. Is this Skippy peanut butter plant really that different? Well, yes and no. What is different about the Best Foods plant in Little Rock is not the "what" but the "how." This plant, like any other plant, has jobs that have to get done, production schedules that have to be met, and reports that have to be sent to the home office. As you walk through the plant, you see people operating machines, taking breaks, and talking. On the surface, it is pretty much the average production facility. There is one difference, however: this plant in Little Rock consistently has had the highest levels of productivity within the corporation.

Within this plant, a workforce of slightly more than one hundred people produces the best product in the world — Skippy peanut butter. Furthermore, they do it better than anyone else in the company! The people working in Little Rock take pride in their operations, take pride in their product, and take pride in being the best. There are just eight managers overall and no first line supervisors. (A goal for the future is to develop a system requiring only three managers.) Work behavior is determined by and governed by the people responsible for producing the products. Put simply, there is a high level of commitment, loyalty, and responsibility on the part of everyone. Sound too good to be true?

POSITION INFORMATION

The current entry positions involve openings in the roasting/ sorting and process packaging areas. The roast/sort tasks involve roasting, blanching, sorting and picking peanuts. The process/packing tasks involve grinding peanuts, blending the ingredients, and packaging the final product. Both jobs demand constant vigilance and monitoring of automated machinery. Employees are in charge of the operations in their assigned area including maintaining and adjusting machines as well as taking complete responsibility when problems occur. Most tasks here entail a great deal of tedious and rigorous attention to cleanliness. Employees are expected to maintain their areas and machines at the highest level of sanitation.

New employees will be working the second shift, from 3 P.M. to 1:30 A.M. Four nights per week is normal, however, weekend work is often required. Schedules and work rules frequently undergo change as employees and other conditions may demand.

The method of management at Best Foods is very unusual and this demands a special kind of employee. Employees here assume a great deal more responsibility for their work than in most any other plant. We expect people to monitor their own performance, and they are, therefore, accountable for their own success. This kind of situation demands that people here are responsible, work extremely well with their co-workers, and be capable of self-discipline. Employees participate in determining their own work rules and policies by organizing and meeting in teams. It is important that all employees take an active part in their groups, feel comfortable speaking in meetings, and establish close working relationships with their fellow employees.

In return, employees of Best Foods enjoy a level of independence and satisfaction rarely found in business today.

Exhibit 2.5   Position Information   Source: Best Foods Co.

Creating a Miracle

The Best Foods plant in Little Rock originated not from any radical ideas but from the desire to create a better way to be competitive. It was undertaken by a quite traditional organization, CPC International. As we observe about each of the companies in this chapter, what makes this Skippy plant operate effectively is not just one thing. It is a web of coordinated, well-thought-out ideas that have been pulled together into the high-productivity operation that exists today.

When the plant in Little Rock was first being conceptualized, there was one overriding belief. According to Larry Shearon, the current plant manager, the belief was, "If the plant was to function effectively, the social and technical systems had to be developed together." That is, equal emphases had to be given to advanced manufacturing processes and to the human part of the organization that ultimately determined the productivity of the total system. Further, the technical and social considerations needed to evolve jointly and interactively. To create a miracle, one must have both an idea or philosophy and action. We will view the development of both in Little Rock.

Basic Management Principles

In the development of the actual physical operating environment at Little Rock, several management principles were thought to be basic to the success of the operation. These principles are:

- Work groups are defined as teams with responsibility for multiple functions.
- Work elements are configured as tasks to be done rather than jobs.
- Compensation should be in the form of a salary rather than hourly wages.

- Salary levels should be based on knowledge of tasks rather than on current work.
- Traditional functions and responsibilities of first line supervision rest in the teams.
- Committees should be responsible for reviewing the practices and procedures at the plant.

The Operating System

To make operational the basic principles, certain underlying values needed to transcend the actual work environment. These were the elements of openness, equality, and equity. Whereas most organizations strive for better communication, the basic requirement at Little Rock is open, meaningful communication. There is a free flow of communication and information throughout the organization. Further, decisions are made by the individuals or teams most directly involved in the decisions and these individuals or teams have a direct interaction with the plant manager. Finally, the relationship of equity to performance was developed through the gain-sharing program.

With the underlying essentials in place, the actual work environment had two issues remaining: actual production and plant operation. The actual production is a function of the immediate work group, which is concerned with the structuring of work, accomplishing operational tasks, and the carrying out of requisite managerial activities. The general plant operation is a function of the plant activity board or councils, which are concerned with coordinating activities between work teams, resolving disputes, long range planning, and the general developmental activities within the plant.

Actual work within the plant is assigned to teams of people. In turn, each work team is accountable for accomplishing its responsibilities. There are no jobs per se, just tasks that have to be accomplished. Workers are thoroughly briefed on every aspect of plant operation. They understand production, costs, demand and distribution. Work teams meet and otherwise take care of their managerial functions in office areas within the plant.

Within many companies, jobs end up being thought of as good jobs or bad jobs. At this Skippy plant, there are tasks and all have to be accomplished. Therefore, team members rotate tasks within the domain of their team's decision-making. Every team member has the chance to perform the interesting tasks, as well as the obligation to share the mundane or less pleasant tasks. Everyone does everything.

Each team member at some point also assumes, on a rotating basis, one of the coordinator roles, which is performed in addition to the member's regular work. The coordinators perform what would be classified as managerial functions in most other companies. Coordinators assign jobs to individuals, counsel deviant individuals, are responsible for maintenance and safety, and so forth. It becomes obvious that there are no boring or dead end jobs here.

The employees at Little Rock are all paid on salary. The salaries are based upon a worker's knowledge and skills that are objectively tested and evaluated. The plant's thirteen step-by-step levels of career development are pursued at the individual's own pace. The philosophy at Little Rock reinforces the idea that "allowing people to grow does not mean you force them to grow."

Effectively performing tasks presents one level of difficulty, but a far greater degree of complexity is encountered in coordinating work teams and guiding plant operations. To achieve this end, four major operating committees govern the overall plant operations in Little Rock. The Social System Support Task Force provides the legislative activities within the plant, and develops and interprets plant norms. The Advanced Certification Board develops certification procedures and training programs. The Plant Review Board recommends disciplinary actions for violations of the code of conduct. And, the Management Council functions like a board of directors by reviewing and approving the activities of the other three operating committees. The composition of each of the operating committees varies, but the key element is that they are operated either solely by representatives of the work groups or jointly by work group representatives and management.

The reasons for the past successes of the Little Rock plant will be the same reasons for its future successes. Larry Shearon points out that "management responsibility is a gray area that keeps moving. Management sets the context or tone of how the plant operates. The people are what make it happen." The operations of Best Foods, Little Rock plant have changed since the plant's inception in 1974, and they will continue to change into the foreseeable future. The things that will not change, though, are being the best and remaining the best.

Freedom and Respect for the Individual
Are the Best Motivators
Kollmorgen Corporation

The Kollmorgen Corporation is a diversified technology company with sales of over $300 million. At Kollmorgen, the emphasis is not just on technological leadership, but more strikingly, on attempting to be "first to the market with the best." While these are ambitious goals, what makes this particular enterprise interesting is that it is engaged in businesses that are primarily related to the highly-competitive electronics industry. Kollmorgen is affected by the ups and downs of its business, just like its competitors are. But unlike many of its rivals, it seems to be able to come back faster and stronger. To understand the strength of Kollmorgen today, one only needs to take a look backward.

About twenty years ago, Bob Swiggett, now chairman of the board, and Jim Swiggett, now CEO, discovered what really made their organization tick. At that time, Kollmorgen was implementing an advanced computer system and was being advised by one of the leading experts on production control from the Harvard Business School. The system was supposed to bring Kollmorgen bravely into the new era of competition. Instead, the system not only failed, but failed dismally. Bob Swiggett recounts: "Statistically we got everything we wanted. We could spit out printouts that would cover the walls in about 15 minutes. The computer worked beautifully, but company performance, if anything, got worse. Foremen were preoccupied with printouts instead of people. Managers spent time worrying about internal systems instead of our customers. People couldn't relate to those printouts, and they resented the control."

Indeed, what the Swiggetts realized was that the basis for success in their industry, innovation and customer satisfaction, was correlated with how well they utilized the people within their company. What the Swiggetts also came to appreciate was what successful military leaders have always known: Armies are made up of individual people. Technology changes the way battles are fought, but people determine who the ultimate winners and losers are.

The computer system was eventually scrapped and teams were once again used as the primary operating unit. The result was that both performance and productivity soared almost immediately and continued to do so for more than a decade. Bob Swiggett comments, "People like to play in a game, to play hard, and bet on the score of the game. Happy, highly motivated players who believe in their game and who understand what they have to do to win will outperform — by a factor of 2-to-1 — unhappy, poorly motivated players who don't understand or know the score of their game." How did Kollmorgen put together a winning team with motivated players?

The direction for the company was set when all of the events and circumstances that were associated with past successes were methodically examined. This process resulted in distilling all important management thoughts and experiences at Kollmorgen and then drafting them into a formal document.

KOLLMORGEN PHILOSOPHY

Management systems and employee motivation may be just as important to a company's success as new technology or fast growing markets; innovation in this area of "software" may be just as important as innovation in product hardware. These things play a vital part in attracting and holding the good people who make everything happen in a growing business.

We have assembled our thoughts on these subjects in the statement on the following four pages, and we urge you to read it carefully. We think it is our key competitive weapon.

Large companies grow much more slowly and create jobs at a slower pace than small companies. Frequently this is so because, as a business grows larger, its founders often turn their main efforts from building the business to controlling and managing risk. We are determined at Kollmorgen not to let caution stifle enterprise.

Our objective is to double sales and earnings every four years. We are confident that we have created product market positions that will let us meet this objective. Our job is to be sure that we are developing the organization, the people, and the systems that will support this rate of growth for the foreseeable future. Hence our intense interest in what makes organizations tick.

Robert L. Swiggett
Robert L. Swiggett
Chairman of the Board

Exhibit 2.6   The Kollmorgen Philosophy   Source: *Kollmorgen Corp.*

Today, this formal document is the Kollmorgen corporate philosophy, the preamble of which is shown in Exhibit 2.6. With the completion of the philosophy, all that remained was creating the actions that would give the philosophy vitality.

Rules for the Road

Bob Swiggett works hard at promoting the Kollmorgen way of life through "road shows" and "Kolture workshops." In these sessions, the precepts of Kollmorgen are continually presented and reinforced. The Kollmorgen belief system is predicated upon the need to bring everyone into contact with the realities of their operating environment: that is, in both positive and negative terms, creating an understanding of what the free market means for company prosperity.

Perhaps the most pervasive and fundamental element within the Kollmorgen philosophy itself is the idea that the organization functions most effectively when it is built on mutual self-respect and trust. In day-to-day terms, this means that corporate values have to be honored, but, equally important, individual values must also be respected. This mutual self-respect is created by fostering open, honest relationships, or as Jack Youngblood, president of the Electro-Optical Division, puts it, by maintaining a "transparent organization." This transparency is attained by making sure that "there are no information monopolies — everybody knows everything." Bob Swiggett elaborates: "The only way people get into trouble, really, is by surprising other people. They don't get into trouble by saying, 'Hey look we've got a problem here.'"

Being open and honest are laudable characteristics, but in and of themselves they are not necessarily qualities that lead to success. The real challenge was how to put the Kollmorgen philosophy into action. Taking the Kollmorgen philosophy on paper and turning it into reality involved two major undertakings: (1) having people understand what being the best really means and (2) having people want to be the best.

Bob Swiggett points out the difficulty of the first proposition by observing, "Few people have ever really been number one. Not many people have ever really been at the top of their class. Most guys are not comfortable with being charged with being number one. You've got the charge: 'Be number one.' But people say, 'Wait a minute. I don't know how to do that.' It's not natural to think you can make it to number one." One of the most difficult aspects of this first endeavor is making sure *everyone*, up, down, and across the organization, understands what being number one feels like.

Bob Swiggett recognizes the significance of this problem, especially as it relates to his own organization, when he pointedly comments, "Look at the janitor. He's forty years old and still a janitor. He really hasn't had a great number of rewarding, 'number one' experiences in his life. His life has stopped. He doesn't have enough money, he has too many kids, his wife is nagging him. But this guy could be a member of a number one team and get a huge charge out of it. I think that's what we try to do. We have to try to tell them 'you're part of this, you're getting part of the winnings, you're part of this team.'" Creating self-worth and an understanding of what peak performance means is valuable, but creating a desire to have peak performance as a way of life is a very different kind of challenge.

How does Kollmorgen make sure that people want to do their best? Primarily by removing the impediments. Kollmorgen tries to let individuals do the things they are supposed to be doing. Most often this means focusing on simple, but essential, things. For example, the work itself, in contrast to paperwork (which is often justified in the name of control), is emphasized. Likewise, the distance between people, psychological as well physical, is reduced so that communication and information interchange is maximized. Finally, personal relationships are seen as key to defining the extent to which Kollmorgen is successful or just exists. Jack Youngblood comments, "You have to click with people; the boxes and lines are secondary."

What goes on in Jack Youngblood's division pretty much reflects what might be considered typical at Kollmorgen. An open-door policy prevails, up to and including the president Jack Youngblood himself. In addition, Jack Youngblood has a brown bag lunch each month that everyone is invited to attend. There are no time cards and everyone works on a variation of flextime. In keeping with Kollmorgen's basic precepts, individuals not only receive competitive wages or salaries, but they can also get a piece of the action and earn a bonus based on their productivity. Most importantly, however, only those with increases in productivity reap the rewards of a bonus. And, when an individual's career at Kollmorgen comes to an end, the relationship is not abruptly terminated. Instead, the individual is phased out. During their last few years, individual employees spend increasingly less time on the job and more time in public service activities such as teaching or volunteer work. Thus, when employees are finishing at Kollmorgen, they are commencing new careers. This far-sighted approach not only fills a potential void in what was the working life of the individual, but at the same time also provides useful services to the community at large. At Kollmorgen much more than the principles of textbook management are used.

In addition to what has been written, there is much more to Kollmorgen — enough to write a book about. At Kollmorgen, life is kept simple and in focus. So simple and straightforward is it, in fact, that most people overlook the reasons for Kollmorgen's past successes. This irony is perceived by Bob Swiggett when he remarks, "People lie, they cheat, they steal, they rip off your car radio. You don't have to set up your business like it is in the outside world. You want people to feel as free from threat as they do in their own bedrooms. We just assume that everybody's honest, and we run the business that way. And people rise to this. But the devil's out there, and he's always whispering in the ear of some manager, 'Hey you've got to control these suckers or they'll run away from you.' So we can't even give away the secret of our success, because most people think it's crap."

If You Don't Live It, You Don't Believe It [1]
The ServiceMaster Company

ServiceMaster is a company most of us are familiar with through its home-cleaning business. But it is much more. It is a company that is not just big, but one that dominates its industry. It has kept a return on equity of about 40 percent and a double-digit sales growth for the past decade. It does so by doing exactly what its name says — by providing service. When ServiceMaster does a job, it doesn't merely do a good job; it does it as well as it can be done. As Dave Baseler, vice-president of marketing services, says, "Whatever it takes, we're here to serve."

The growth of ServiceMaster has come by rigorously following the set of objectives shown in Exhibit 2.7. While highly unorthodox in most corporate circles, these objectives have been responsible for the unparalleled growth of ServiceMaster. Probably the most remarkable feature is that profits are rated last among the objectives. Although rated last, the importance of profits is not diminished for ServiceMaster. It is well understood that profits must be achieved to maintain and enhance the current position of the company. As Ken Wessner,

[1] Quote of ServiceMaster Founder Marion Wade

The
Objectives of
ServiceMaster

To honor God
in all we do
To help people
develop
To pursue excellence
To grow profitably

Source: *ServiceMaster's 1986 Annual Report*

Exhibit 2.7   ServiceMaster's Objectives

Chairman of the Board, elaborates, "We perceive profitable growth not as an end in itself, but as a means through which to achieve other, more visionary objectives."

From an overall perspective, perhaps the most uncommon aspect of ServiceMaster is its concern for people. Many companies have gone beyond what can be termed simple personnel administration and have embraced human resource management which endeavors to take a more systematic view of their employees. ServiceMaster has removed many of the pretentious trappings that have tended to develop in other companies. In fact, ServiceMaster has simplified and clarified the role of this function. People are not treated as resources like machinery, inventory, or money. At ServiceMaster, the people are the organization. That idea is central to every person making a decision.

The person in charge of taking care of the people in the organization is the vice-president for people.[2] Vice-president for people Bill Hargreaves looks after not just the needs of the company but also the welfare of the people and how they fit into the organization. The key to the growth of the ServiceMaster Company is that it provides a vehicle for people to grow to whatever they can *be*.

People = Performance

What separates ServiceMaster from many other companies in its concern for people is what the company gives. It gives people a sense of value, a workplace as free of traditional negative qualities as possible, and a positive environment (a first for many people) which promotes superior service and innovation.

[2] It was pointed out to me that it is not the vice-president *of* people, but *for* people.

What ServiceMaster instills into the individuals that comprise the company is pride. Pride in their job and pride in working for ServiceMaster. This task is accomplished by involving everyone in the business. Every manager starts out at ServiceMaster by performing basic duties. If you are a manager of housekeeping at a hospital, for instance, then you actually perform the same duties as your subordinates. As a senior officer, Alexander Balc, explains, "Our willingness to roll up our sleeves and be part of the process communicates to people that they are important and there is value [in their jobs]."

The final element is that ServiceMaster not only tries to remove much of the negative circumstances present in other companies but, perhaps most importantly, also tries to create a positive work system — a system that not only allows, but promotes, individual growth. How is this done? In two ways, first by the individual manager and then by the organization itself. What ServiceMaster does is make a team. This is not the futile "team-building" exercises that other companies many times undertake, but an honest-to-goodness team based on individual concern. When the team is put together, members are taught the rules of the game.

What does it mean to be a manager of a team at ServiceMaster? Two instances will typify what it means to be a manager. In the first situation, a manager had a deaf person come into his work area. What was his first action? Taking courses in signing. Not a normal reaction at most companies, but a rather ordinary one at ServiceMaster. The second situation concerns a manager who was new to a position at a hospital. He was told early on to watch out for John the floor finisher who was seen as a difficult worker. This was a cue to the manager that the situation should be looked into, rather than accepting the advice at face value. Very quickly, the manager inquired into why John was always in trouble. He was a problem employee not because he was basically a bad person but because he had too many abilities that were not being utilized. Today, John works for ServiceMaster as a divisional vice-president in their East Coast business. ServiceMaster managers excel in, and perhaps even thrive on, converting difficult situations into positive results.

The second situation with John the floor finisher in the preceding paragraph, I believe, points out why ServiceMaster has been a highly productive and profitable company. In many organizations, John would be classified as a marginal performer and perhaps be a disciplinary problem. The consequences: (1) low productivity from John, (2) decreased productivity for the manager, because John is taking up inordinate amounts of the manager's time, and (3) actual increases in cost (read that as decreased profits) because of disciplinary actions that have to be taken. John's manager at ServiceMaster spent whatever time he would have spent if the negative relationship had been maintained. But instead, following the objectives of trying to develop each individual not only increased productivity in his own work area, but enhanced the long-term interests of the organization.

As a final step, ServiceMaster teaches the rules of the game, much as other companies in this chapter do, through its tailored training program. Each person knows what is necessary and important, whether the person is just starting out as a new manager or is a vice-president. ServiceMaster has developed its own MBA style program so that both the individual and the company can stay on the success track.

At ServiceMaster, it is evident that the company does not take the easy way, to which any ServiceMaster manager would probably respond, "But it is the right way." The motto at ServiceMaster might well be "Difficult situations we can handle immediately; impossible situations take a bit longer." What also becomes equally evident when viewing ServiceMaster is that the apparent altruism driving corporate actions is being converted into real profits.

Back to the Basics Has Never Been More Basic
Lands' End

Lands' End was started about 20 years ago as a sailing supply business. As requests for related products increased, Lands' End slowly moved away from the original business. By 1977, sailboat equipment was dropped completely and Lands' End became a mail order merchant of sports and casual clothing. To classify Lands' End as just a mail order company, though, would be a misnomer. Lands' End is changing the concept of mail order. It violates old rules and makes new ones.

The growth of Lands' End during the last decade can only be described as meteoric. It has grown from about 50 to about 1,500 regular full-time employees and to almost twice that number during the peak season. During the same time period, facilities expanded by more than ten-fold. In 1989, the company rang up nearly $500 million in annual sales, with a profit margin far in excess of the industry average.

Service and Quality Par Excellence

Some companies are described as having an uncompromising attitude toward quality and service, but Lands' End goes beyond that and can only be described as *absolutely* dedicated to quality and service. Lands' End customers get exactly what they want or their money is returned, and that's a guarantee. The principles of doing business which guide corporate actions at Lands' End are shown in Exhibit 2.8.

The reason for the Lands' End success is not very complicated. In fact, it is rather simple. Dick Anderson, president and chief operating officer, probably sums it up best when he states, "We're not out to make a sale but to make a relationship." This relationship is no ordinary relationship as Exhibit 2.9, a letter from a customer, indicates. Perhaps more significant, though,

PRINCIPLES OF DOING BUSINESS

Principle 1.
We do everything we can to make our products better. We improve material, and add back features and construction details that others have taken out over the years. We never reduce the quality of a product to make it cheaper.

Principle 2.
We price our products fairly and honestly. We do not, have not, and will not participate in the common retailing practice of inflating mark-ups to set up a future phoney "sale."

Principle 3.
We accept any return, for any reason, at any time. Our products are guaranteed. No fine print. No arguments. We mean exactly what we say: GUARANTEED. PERIOD.

Principle 4.
We ship faster than anyone we know of. We ship items in stock the day after we receive the order. At the height of the last Christmas season the longest time an order was in the house was 36 hours, excepting monograms which took another 12 hours.

Principle 5.
We belive that what is best for our customer is best for all of us.

Everyone here understands that concept. Our sales and service people are trained to know our products, and to be friendly and helpful. They are urged to take all the time necessary to take care of you. We even pay for your call, for whatever reason you call.

Principle 6.
We are able to sell at lower prices because we have eliminated middlemen; because we don't buy branded merchandise with high protected mark-ups; and because we have placed our contracts with manufacturers who have proved that they are cost conscious and efficient.

Principle 7.
We are able to sell at lower prices because we operate efficiently. Our people are hard working, intelligent and share in the success of the company.

Principle 8.
We are able to sell at lower prices because we support no fancy emporiums with their high overhead. Our main location is in the middle of a 40-acre cornfield in rural Wisconsin. We still operate our first location in Chicago's Near North tannery district.

Source: Lands' End Co.

Exhibit 2.8   Lands' End Principles of Doing Business

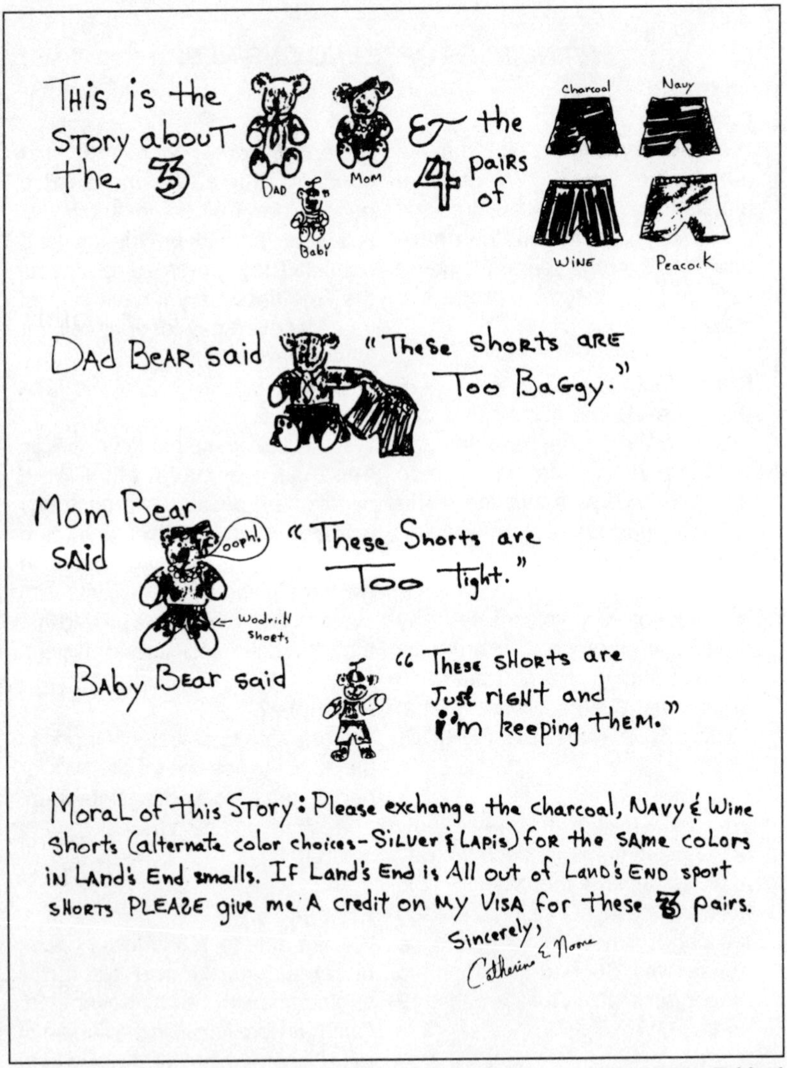

Exhibit 2.9 Customer Letter to Lands' End   Source: Lands' End News Tabloid

this philosophy seems to carry through to most other company activities as well.

Just as service and quality ultimately end with the customer, they must invariably begin with the people who make up the company. Further, just as Lands' End has defined what a mail order business is in its own terms, it has also defined what managing means in its own terms. As one walks into the facilities, one quickly gets the impression that Lands' End is different. Within each major operations area, signs wish a "Happy Birthday" to employees whose birthdays fall on that day. As one walks a bit farther, one sees a lunch and break area with vending machines. This area too is quite different. Trees are interspersed among tables and chairs and all are within a lighted atrium.

What the preceding depiction exemplifies is what Lands' End does best as a company — it pays attention. Instead of focusing on high visibility activities, it is generally more useful to focus on less obvious and more mundane activities to discover what really is important. To illustrate the attention that Lands' End pays at all levels of its operations, one only needs to look at a position that is generally quite low in the hierarchy of most companies — the telephone operator. The person who starts as a telephone operator at Lands' End receives two full weeks of training. Further, each year, veteran operators are required to take 72 hours of training on Lands' End product lines. One might ask why so much training for such a typically low-level position? At Lands' End, no position or person is unimportant. Everyone is listened to and everyone adds to the overall productivity.

Lands' End training for telephone people is put to good use. The company recognizes that rather than having a dull, repetitive job, these people are the first vital link to service and quality for its customers. Telephone operators have full access to product and inventory information and customer histories, so they can answer almost any question that customers ask. "Last year I bought a tweed sport coat. What slacks will match it?" or "I would like to buy something for my wife. What do you suggest?" are run-of-the-mill questions for most of the company's operators. If the need arises, the operator can even get up and look at the actual merchandise. Thus, the telephone operator at Lands' End is as much an advisor as anything else!

Simplicity Is a Virtue (and a Competitive Advantage)

At Lands' End, a few simple rules guide management actions. These rules are: (1) Put people where they are most productive; (2) Listen to what people incumbent in the job are saying (after all, they are the experts); (3) Remove the impediments to doing a good job.

One example of how these rules are put into practice at Lands' End is through a job enrollment program. The job enrollment program allows individuals to try out other jobs within the company while still on their own jobs. If an opening occurs (vacation, for example), an individual can try out the job. People eventually settle where they feel most comfortable and can do their best work.

Then, the management at Lands' End does what it does best — pays attention. From the top of the organization to the bottom, managers listen carefully to what everyone says. Comments, problems, and frustrations are thought through, and any existing impediments to doing a good job are mitigated or removed entirely.

What do people mean at Lands' End? Earlier, we observed the attention paid to the telephone operators on their jobs. Several other examples point out what its people mean to the company.

- In a recent Christmas issue of the *News Tabloid*, the Lands' End in-house newspaper, everyone who works for the company was listed. Most notably, the name of Gary Comer, the chairman of the board, appeared right along with all the other individuals (somewhere near the middle of the list) who contribute to the Lands' End success.

- Package inserts, such as the one shown in Exhibit 2.10, are sent out with every order. They bear the picture of an employee along with a short quote describing that employee's job and how it affects the customer.
- An individual and that person's job are spotlighted in the monthly catalog/magazine sent to the customers.

The question "What do people mean at Lands' End?" was asked at the beginning of the paragraph. Like most other things at Lands' End, the answer is simple. Everything.

"I see to it that you get your catalog."

"We really try hard to fill your requests promptly and correctly, whatever they are—whether you've moved and have a new address, or are asking for a new catalog the first time. We try to treat you the way we'd want to be treated ourselves.

"One tip I can give you is this: if you're sending an address label for a correction, it's a good idea to specify exactly how you'll want it to read. That way, we'll be sure to get it right."

Nancy Neu

Exhibit 2.10   Lands' End Package Insert

Meeting the Japanese Challenge
Motorola, Inc.

At Motorola there is an informal policy of continuing employment. After ten years of service, an employee cannot be terminated without the approval of Bob Galvin, chairman of the board. The company is quite diligent in its efforts to provide job security for all its regular employees. During the past decade, while Motorola was keeping its promise, some of our largest corporations have done just the opposite and gotten rid of many of their employees. Not just a few but, in some cases, tens of thousands of people. Think about that.

The real meaning of the Motorola policy is not that Motorola is guaranteeing lifetime employment, but that Motorola is guaranteeing it will provide better management. What has been the effect of Motorola's guarantee of better management? The results seem to be pretty clear. In the decade since 1976, Motorola has tripled its sales and doubled its profits. Today, Motorola has more than 90,000 employees located in 28 countries around the world. Further, Motorola currently defines itself as the world leader in mobile land communication, and at the same time, it has also been proclaimed one of the 100 best companies to work for in the United States.

Underlying Motorola's success is a well-thought-out plan of action. The focus of the firm is defined by the "keys to success": key beliefs, key goals, and key initiatives. As we view these "keys" in Exhibit 2.11, we can clearly see that within each key area people and their relationship to the organization are included. Perhaps the most important observation is that Motorola realizes that the key to high quality products and a positive customer orientation is having truly motivated and properly informed employees.

Let me repeat that again. The Motorola system revolves around the concept of allowing its people to be motivated and keeping them informed.

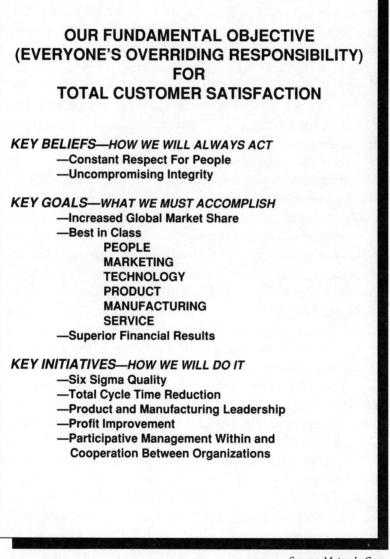

**OUR FUNDAMENTAL OBJECTIVE
(EVERYONE'S OVERRIDING RESPONSIBILITY)
FOR
TOTAL CUSTOMER SATISFACTION**

KEY BELIEFS—HOW WE WILL ALWAYS ACT
—Constant Respect For People
—Uncompromising Integrity

KEY GOALS—WHAT WE MUST ACCOMPLISH
—Increased Global Market Share
—Best in Class
    PEOPLE
    MARKETING
    TECHNOLOGY
    PRODUCT
    MANUFACTURING
    SERVICE
—Superior Financial Results

KEY INITIATIVES—HOW WE WILL DO IT
—Six Sigma Quality
—Total Cycle Time Reduction
—Product and Manufacturing Leadership
—Profit Improvement
—Participative Management Within and
  Cooperation Between Organizations

Exhibit 2.11   Motorola's Keys to Success   *Source: Motorola Corp.*

Building Blocks

Two key ingredients provide the basis so that Motorola can carry out its commitments. The first component is the ambitious and far-reaching Participative Management Process, referred to as the PMP. Education, the second component, reflects the company's dedication to development of the individuals who make up Motorola. Currently 2.4 percent of Motorola's annual payroll budget is allocated to advancing knowledge and skills.

Participative Management Process. The Participative Management Process (PMP) provides Motorola with a perspective that is quite different from mainstream corporate America. Perhaps the most interesting (or perhaps refreshing?) part of Motorola's style is that managers are required to be frank, even to the point of admitting past errors. The PMP rests on four cardinal principles, which are shown in Figure 2.1. The principles are management commitment, participation, communication, and trust.

The most critical of these principles is management commitment, because it is central to the success of the three other principles. Motorola clearly realizes agreement can exist without action. Thus, mere verbal commitment is only a very small first step. To be successful it is understood that commitment must have vitality. Motorola managers, therefore, lead by example.

A second principle is that of participation. In many organizations, participation takes on appearance more than substance. At Motorola, a basic belief is that individual commitment and shared ideas have a far greater impact on the prosperity of the company than the contributions of any individual manager. As a consequence, ideas and an understanding of the job are viewed not just as being important but as being a valuable organizational resource.

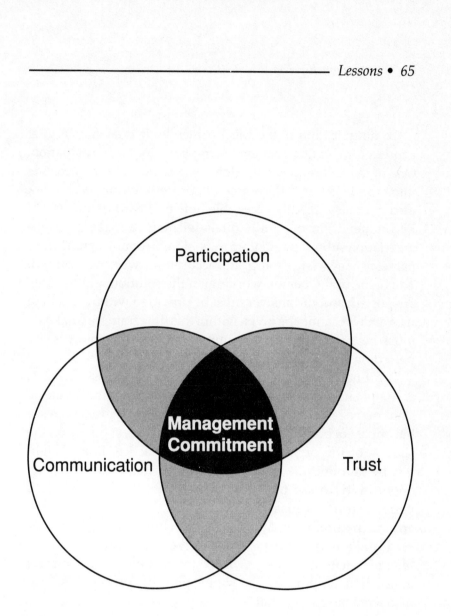

Figure 2.1   Motorola's Participative Management Process Principles

Communication is the third principle. It is seen as a vital process for creating and enhancing meaningful participation. One of the techniques that Motorola uses to set this principle into motion is the "I Recommend" process. Within each work area, there is a readily accessible bulletin board displaying "I Recommend" forms. Individuals wishing to make a recommendation submit one of the forms, signing or not signing their names as they wish. Prompt and accurate answers are required. The name of the person working on the solution and the date are posted, and the answer must be provided within 72 hours. If an answer cannot be given within this time frame, a final date must be provided. All recommendations and answers are posted on the "I Recommend" board.

The final principle in the PMP process is trust. Trust is accomplished in two ways: line of sight and equity. Line of sight management at Motorola means that individuals can see the impact of both their actions and the actions of others on the success of the organization. In actual practice, line of sight revolves around the use of teams so that individuals have an opportunity to see that their actions can affect their team's performance. Because PMP teams are small and structured around naturally separate work functions, line of sight is readily apparent. Line of sight, however, goes farther than just the immediate work group. The operating environment is set up so that employees can judge policies, procedures, and managers based on what is actually done, rather than just on what is said. The second element in developing trust is equity. Equity is addressed primarily through a corporate bonus structure. Rewards are based on skill levels, experience, and education and are made as close in time as possible to actual performance. Thus, a sense of sharing and sharing fairly is achieved throughout the organization.

William Grundstrom, manager of client services, capsulizes

the PMP as a process where "the concept of participative management was based on an understanding that, for Motorola to become more successful, employees at every level of the organization would have to become more involved with the company, more interested in where it was going, and more excited about contributing to its future." More interestingly, he depicts the PMP as a process through which "Motorola was able to get teams to function together in a systematic way, without sacrificing the welfare of the individual."

Education. The second building block is the educational process that has evolved at Motorola. Being in the highly competitive and changeable electronics industry demands that the company's technical expertise be continually updated. However, Motorola goes far beyond the minimum technical requirements. Motorola has created an advanced learning environment to update technical skills, organizational skills, and reinforce basic values. As changing technology and world-wide competitiveness demand more from companies intent upon being world-class, the Motorola educational process enables its employees, including senior executives, engineers, and production floor workers, to continually upgrade their skills and remain optimally productive.

How do you become successful at Motorola? Exhibit 2.12 shows the path in manufacturing management. Motorola has equally clear paths for other areas of its organization, too. All of the skills necessary for success are mapped out for an individual to follow. Training does not take place on a haphazard basis but through a systematic approach which benefits the individual and ultimately the organization as a whole.

Today Motorola is meeting the Japanese challenge by trying to better understand its competitors and customers. But it is also meeting a far greater challenge that will ultimately

Manufacturing Operation Management Development Guide

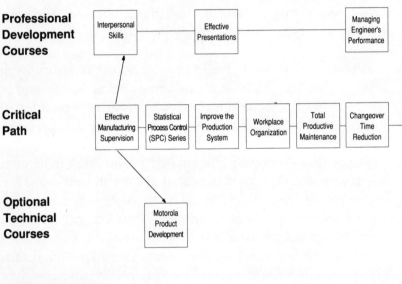

First Level Manager

Professional Development Courses

Interpersonal Skills — Effective Presentations — Managing Engineer's Performance

Critical Path

Effective Manufacturing Supervision — Statistical Process Control (SPC) Series — Improve the Production System — Workplace Organization — Total Productive Maintenance — Changeover Time Reduction

Optional Technical Courses

Motorola Product Development

Course Legend:
Critical Path Courses —

Effective Manufacturing Supervision (MFG 240)
  3¹/2 Days
Statistical Process Control (SPC) Series
  Core I (SPC 360-372) - 3 Days
  Core II (SPC 374-386) - 5 Days
  Core III (SPC 388-396) - 9 Days
Improve the Production System (MFG 341) - 2 Days
Workplace Organization (MFG 342) - 2 Days
Total Productive Maintenance (MFG 343) - 2 Days
Changeover Time Reduction (MFG 344) - 2 Days

Group Technology / Material Flow (MFG 345) - 2 Days
Asset Management (FIN 103) - 2¹/2 Days
Manufacturing Cycle Management (MFG 327) - 3 Days
Leveling Production Schedules (MFG 346) - 2 Days
Pull Production System (MFG 347) - 2 Days
Project Planning/Project Control (ENG 111/ENG 131)
  2 Days +1 Day
Successful Negotiator (PUR 200) - 3 Days
Motorola Management Institute (MMI 100) - 2 Weeks

Exhibit 2.12   Manufacturing Operations Management Development Guide

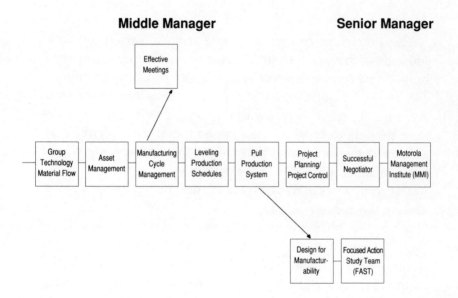

Professional Development Courses —

Interpersonal Skills (MGT 106) - 2 Days
Effective Presentations (MFG 201) - 2 Days
Managing Engineer's Performance (ENG 119) - 2 Days
Effective Meetings (MGT 202) - 2 Days

Optional Technical Courses —

Mototola Product Development (ENG 110) - 3 Days
Design for Manufacturability (ENG 123) - 2 Days
Focused Action Study Team (FAST) (ENG 130) - 3 Days

Source: Motorola Training and Education Center, Programs and Services 1988

determine its destiny, not for just next year or the year after but into the new millennium. The ultimate challenge for Motorola is not the Japanese but one of understanding itself and what really makes its own organization run well.

Final Comment

The preceding companies come from a variety of backgrounds with respect to size, industry, and even basic orientations. Some companies seem to be driven by altruistic motives and others are quite pragmatic. As diverse as these companies are, though, there is much more commonality among them than there is to most of their contemporaries. They have all arrived at the same focal point, even though they started out from considerably different perspectives.

The companies in this chapter are not put forth as paragons. They make mistakes. As Dave Baseler of ServiceMaster puts it, "We've probably made more mistakes than right decisions." At times, some of these companies even perform poorly, as Kollmorgen has in the mid-1980s. What sets them apart is their ability to move rapidly and correct errors when they are recognized. When things start to go wrong, the tendency in many organizations is to act like airplanes running out of gas, throwing out everything that isn't bolted down, and even some of the things that are.

CHAPTER THREE

Actions Speak Louder than Words

———

Actions Speak Louder than Words

Endurance is the crowning quality,
And patience all the passion of great hearts
                              —James Russell Lowell

W HEN we look at high-performance companies, it is very easy to
admire their accomplishments. These companies are often
marvelled at in the belief that they can never really be duplicated. Many of these organizations are even treated as aberra-
tions from what is considered to be "normal." Rather than ab-
errations, these companies can best be described as prototypes
which develop their own rules as they go along.

This chapter examines what the successful, high-performance companies actually do and identifies universal behaviors
or principles under which these companies seem to operate.
These principles represent how these companies have achieved
success in the past and also equally depict a working blueprint
for their future.

Masters of Paradox

Companies that achieve high levels of performance have
done so primarily by understanding fundamental management paradoxes. They make sense out of contradictory
relationships and outcomes. The principles presented in this

73

chapter resulted as these companies attempted to reconcile paradoxes. In most cases, the recognition did not come as a result of some blinding flash of insight, but more often from blind groping through trial and error. Three paradoxes appear to underlie these principles. These are:

- The paradox of self-defeating success. Early and fast success often blinds a company to the real reasons for that success. Being successful in a market or with a product doesn't mean that the company will remain successful. Continued success can only come because of the organization itself. Only understanding this will allow the right emphases to occur and the correct sequencing of actions to take place so that initial successes can be maintained.

- The paradox of control. When a situation appears to be out of kilter, the first tendency is to tighten the grip, but the real problem is not the day-to-day activities. Daily activities are only a reflection of a system that needs fixing. From an overall perspective, the reality is that greater flexibility at the lower levels of a business leads to greater control, not less. Decision making at the lower levels of the organization is a problem and can be abused only when there is no point of reference for the decision maker.

- The paradox of responsibility. The bad news of this paradox is you *cannot give* responsibility to another. You can try, but frustration and disappointment will only result. The good news is that people *will take* and even relish responsibility. However, people will only take responsibility when they are part of the action, that is, when they are creating something over which they have some control.

Principles for High Performance

Principle 1: Participation, Not Participative Management

Participative management is often interpreted as a sign of advanced thinking in today's companies. When we talk to managers, though, we tend to be confronted by an assortment of images, some positive and some negative, about what participative management is or is not. The circumstance becomes even more confusing when we look at what people are actually doing (especially those who seem to be doing things that are contrary to what they are advocating). Among the companies presented in Chapter 2, and in other high-performance companies, what is emphasized is a no-frills participation rather than some esoteric view. Each company practices its own brand of participation, but, in all cases, what it really comes down to is involving people in the process. Upon observation, what also becomes clearly evident is that any formal approach to management (autocratic versus democratic) becomes a secondary issue when the concern is with high performance. It is the intent that counts and makes the difference.

Lincoln Electric is a company that claims to be autocratic, when in practice the Management Advisory Board has a significant input into what is done in the company. At the other end of the spectrum is the Best Foods plant in Little Rock, Arkansas. When a matter of concern arises at this plant, meetings are called, the issues discussed, and recommendations are made to the plant manager. What these two cases illustrate is that management, whether autocratic or democratic, does not abdicate its management or decision-making responsibilities. What we have are really just two different sides of the same coin. At "autocratic" Lincoln, management goes out of its way to get input. When decisions are made, everyone can live with them. While all employees may not see eye-to-eye on the decisions, they carry them out without hesitation because it is in the best interest of the company and the individuals to do so. At the Best Foods plant, a different process is used but the conclusion is the same. To external observers, Lincoln and Best Foods in Little Rock would appear to be organizations that are vastly different, even poles apart. In the end, though, the net consequences are the same for both.

As was pointed out earlier, high performance is a function of intent rather than style in every case observed. Thus, management style, a much discussed issue in some quarters, becomes essentially a moot point. What does intent mean? It means concern for what is actually going on rather than what should be going on and plugging people into what is happening.

The reality of participation within high-performance companies doesn't mean sharing the power, but that we are all in this together. This is a profound distinction, and this is what intent is. Intent is not, "I am giving you something; be grateful or else I will take it back from you." Instead, it is this: "We all perform different functions. However, all are important to our overall success." Thus, one cannot take an overt process or style developed in one company and put it in place in another company and necessarily have it work, because it probably won't.

Principle 2: Point of Pride

High-performance companies seem to be distinguished in some area — either in providing an advanced product or service, an advanced process, or in understanding a business relationship better than its competitors. The distinguishing factor seems to become a rallying point for employees. More importantly, it tends to become a point of pride for employees. It symbolizes, in a very concrete way, that the efforts they have already expended have been successful.

Each company presented in Chapter 2 has managed to develop some distinguishing factor. Motorola defines itself as the world leader in mobile land communication and the prime mover in the paging business. Lands' End transformed the mail-order business by initiating and perfecting the use of the 800 telephone number. S. C. Johnson is a world leader in aerosol manufacturing and produces 14 percent of all the aerosol packaging used in the world today. Lincoln Electric has a history of knocking far larger competitors out of its markets and in developing productivity rates that are far greater than even those of its nearest competitors.

It is difficult to continually tell people to be excellent without sometimes showing them the results of that excellence. What these companies have done is to make the combined efforts of everyone tangible, so tangible that all can proudly wear the "badge" of their company. The badge of success doesn't say 'I am someone,' but 'I am someone special.'

Principle 3: Develop People (and Never Stop)

I have good news and bad news about education in the United States. The good news is that our educational system is probably the most advanced and widespread system in the world. The bad news is that it doesn't provide what most businesses really need. We teach people about marketing, finance, accounting, operations management, and R&D, but not how to run a business. We teach people about leadership, but not how to lead. We teach people how to make decisions (our quantitative techniques provide us with an unparalleled level of precision), but not how to carry them out. We teach people about strategic management, but not how to compete successfully.

Before I am perceived as railing against the educational establishment, let me say that our current system is doing a pretty good job, because many of these apparent shortcomings are ones that can only be remedied by the organization itself. Education has to be tailor-made to fit the organization. What many companies have learned the hard way is that the best and most valuable people do not always come from the best schools. High-performance companies develop and shape the people in their organizations into what they want and need. Such value can only come from within the organization.

Why does education have to be fit to the organization? Probably the best way to answer the question is with an analogy. A thrust is being made in our educational system to remove illiteracy. One issue being debated is the role of knowledge versus skills. We have been imparting skills at all levels of our educational system — elementary schools, high schools, and in universities at both the undergraduate and graduate levels. Our highly-educated individuals go out and are not productive. Why? Because of organizational illiteracy. This illiteracy occurs because individuals don't understand — except on an individual or political plane — how what they already know fits into their organization. The comment has been made that "no culture exists that is ignorant of its own traditions." This comment is equally applicable to our contemporary companies and, I believe, in a large measure explains why we observe that the book values of some companies are higher than their market values and why these companies eventually become vulnerable and end up as acquisition candidates.

High-performance companies not only fit skills into the organizational context, but more importantly, they impart knowledge about the organization itself. IBM "brainwashes" its employees. The Skippy plant in Little Rock "brainwashes" its employees. Lincoln "brainwashes" its employees. When I use the term "brainwash," it is not the typically negative description; rather, it is a positive attribute of the organization.

Within most companies, people are told what is wrong. In contrast, high-performance companies tell people what is right. All that means is that people know what the company expects and what should be done.

The question has been posed, Why do companies in countries that emphasize management education (Great Britain and the United States) seem not to perform as well as those in countries that do not emphasize management education (West Germany and Japan)? I think the answer is obvious.

Principle 4: Everyone Gets Part of the Winnings

Though difficult to define, one particularly distinctive characteristic of high-performance companies is what their individuals get from the organizations. Individuals tend to receive their winnings at different levels. On one level, everyone gets to feel like they are number one, somehow. This is a psychological winning that everyone receives. While it is self- esteem, it is also more than just self-esteem. It is something that makes all employees, regardless of their immediate job, feel they are important and that they contribute to the success of the company. In addition, and on a much different level, there also is financial equity within the system. Financial sharing is common but not universal. Financial equity is probably the most misunderstood aspect of getting the winnings. It is not money for money's sake. Instead, it symbolizes a successful effort and it equitably represents the extra or extraordinary effort expended. Much like stockholders, employees get a return for their investment. Their investment of time, energy, and effort receives _commensurate_ rewards.

Further, the rewards or winnings relate to the immediate job, as well as to the overall operations of the organization. Process rewards are correlated to everyday activities and are linked with parts of the organization other than immediate job activities. In this way, vital issues like innovation and quality become part of a common routine. The content rewards are directly related to the immediate job. Thus, the reward system connects short-range goals to long-range goals. People do the right things for the right reasons.

Of all the principles in this chapter, this particular one presents the greatest challenge because even though winning occurs on different levels, the levels are interdependent. Consequently, simple actions, such as giving a bonus, may not result in attainment of the desired level of performance but, in fact, may end up reducing it.

Principle 5: Reality Rules

The realities for one company or industry generally are very different from the realities of another. However, there is a collective realization among high-performance companies. The realization relates simply to a fundamental understanding of the realities of doing business. Within these companies, each person is connected to and understands the economic realities of the business. Many companies today do just the opposite and shelter people by not letting them know what is going on — until it is too late.

Just what is it that people in high-performance companies do know or understand?

There is the reality of competition. If we don't do it and do it better, our competitors eventually will. Thus, there is a distinct propensity for action. High-performance companies certainly stop and think. But when the time for action arrives, they act.

There is the reality of productivity. The activities of individuals affect their company far beyond whatever happens to be going on in their immediate job. Each person in a high-performance company realizes that, as individuals, they contribute to the success of the organization. This realization is brought about because each person is plugged into the customers — some more directly than others; understands the industry; and, most of all, appreciates what value really means. They are aware of costs, the unity of operations, and what effectiveness demands at the personal level.

There is the reality of results. What really determines the success of a company are its outcomes not its activities. A fairly accurate observation of most highly performing companies is that they more often use "Management by Principle" rather than "Management by Rule." That means that individual actions are taken in light of the purpose and objectives of the organization, instead of solely going by the book. In other words, when actions are taken, they are meaningful in an organizational sense rather than just empty motions. The operative precept that was advocated in one organization was "Do What's Right!" The effective organizations are vigorous in shifting the focal point from rules and regulations to outcomes.

There is one more reality. Perhaps, it is the most important reality of all. It is the recognition and appreciation of the idea that "If the company does poorly, everyone does poorly." There cannot be winners and losers. Everybody plays on the same team.

Principle 6: Security and Productivity Do Not Conflict

High-performance companies emphasize security for their employees. This does not also mean that inevitably there is complacency, as some people would be quick to point out. What it does mean is that an atmosphere is created that is notably absent of fear. As W. Edwards Deming, perhaps the foremost authority on quality and productivity, suggests, fear has to be driven out of the workplace; fear that a person will be fired or laid-off because of factors beyond the person's control — the economy or even from management itself. Individuals must not be afraid to present a good idea. In some companies, if you come up with a way of eliminating your job, you may also eliminate yourself from the company. This incongruous behavior of punishing a person who has made the company more productive creates tremendous repercussions in every area of the organization. Perhaps the greatest fear of all is that you don't count. When someone finds a better way of doing something or sees an answer to a problem, an all-too-often consequence is that nobody does anything about it, and just as frequently, the person or idea is not even acknowledged. In some large ways and many small ways, people are told they don't count. At times it is unintentional; at other times it is done on purpose. Either way, the result is the same.

Security is provided on many levels. Sometimes it is related to the basic economic aspects of employment. In most high-performance companies, however, there is always more. Security becomes a part of everyday operations. For innovations or improvements to occur as a normal part of activities, there has to be the ability to fail. High-performance companies are characteristically "bad losers" in that respect. It does not mean that people are punished for failing. It means that failure doesn't become an accepted way of life. These companies realize that with failure learning must occur. Failing and learning have value, while failing and forgetting are generally terminal.

Common wisdom relates that fat cats don't hunt. And common wisdom is right in many instances. What we observe in high performers is that rather than being a deterrent to productivity, security has just the opposite effect. It creates an environment where people can learn, grow, and be more productive!

Principle 7: No Jobs, Only Work that Has To Be Done

The accent in productive organizations is on work, not on jobs — the way that work is classified. The focus is centered on tasks, not on turf — the performing and achieving of what has to accomplished. Put simply, the difference is in perspective. While it might be called attitude, or it might even be called motivation, it all means the same thing. The difference in perspectives between high-productivity organizations and their not-so-productive counterparts may be as simple as the answers received when individuals are asked to describe how they do their work. Is the response, "I do a good job" or "I do the best job that I can?"

The latter answer indicates a self-imposed accountability because individuals have a purpose and, therefore, a focal point to use in defining their responsibility. Mark Pastin, one of the savviest of the contemporary business observers, contends "genuine responsibility begins where mere response to a reward system ends." However, he makes the equally important remark that "you cannot be genuinely responsible for something unless you were part of the cause of its happening." Do people in your organization make things happen or do things happen to them? Are they in control or are they being controlled? Control creates responsibility, nothing else.

Some companies today see the key to their productivity problem as too many people. They probably are right. Their solution has been to decrease the number of layers in the organization and make everyone responsible for more than they were previously. The joke is on them. But the joke won't be funny because the punchline will be a lawsuit, poor quality in a product or service, lost customers, or an accident. Why? Because responsibility is being given without control, and it is apparent responsibility, not genuine responsibility. Genuine responsibility means accepting accountability for what I do and also ownership for the blurry area that might belong to someone else.

How can you tell how much responsibility is present in an organization? Answer the following: If safety, for example, is important in your organization, and a top level manager is walking through a plant or office and sees something lying in the walkway, would the manager pick it up? Would a middle level manager pick it up? Would the immediate manager pick it up? If not, why should anyone else?

Principle 8: Some Interactions Are Better than Others

Companies that have had successful long-term track records invariably tend to have good communication between individuals. Again, like the other principles in this chapter, this does not carry the ordinary or expected connotation. These organizations become highly personalized organizations. What we experience is not just feedback — but that somebody is *always* listening.

Along with an active approach to communication, there also tends to be a high degree of information-sharing among individuals. This unity of communication and information in high-performance organizations is not very typical on a wide scale in most other organizations. Information is often treated as a bargaining chip rather than as a resource for the common good. The one who holds the information invariably holds the power. Hence, there are information monopolies. To obtain necessary information one must either outflank, threaten, or overpower the possessor of the wanted information. Time is used poorly, and energy is needlessly expended to get what should be readily available.

Much emphasis is placed on the process of communication among people, and it certainly is important. Only when communication and information are viewed separately, however, are we able to have not only genuine interactions but productive interactions as well. Productive interactions occur when (1) a climate of openness or frankness allows (2) the giving or providing of relevant information (or feelings) and (3) the listening and allowing of input from others. Productive interactions can only occur, though, when people see mutual benefits from a common perspective.

Principle 9: Human Beings Need a Human Scale

How large an operation is the right size? One hundred people? One thousand people? Ten thousand people? How many subordinates should a manager have? Five? Fifty? One hundred? These and other similar questions have been pondered, discussed, and argued. What is the correct answer? All of them are correct. Different companies have come to different conclusions about the right size for the operating environments in their organizations. Each can be correct for their environment. The real question is not how large or how small, but whether people understand the environment in which they must interact. Do they know what is going on, or are they confused, frustrated, and hostile? Are people in the organization truly a part of the action, or are they really just observers of what is going on around them?

Human beings thrive in environments that they can comprehend. When people find it difficult or impossible to grasp what is going on in their surroundings, they don't become involved and usually opt into circumstances that are more comfortable. Put simply, when a working environment is not understandable, alienation can occur and efforts tend to be transferred to areas that can be mastered. What we then observe is a gradual fragmentation of individual activities and interests. The result is an away-from-work life that prospers at the expense of at-work life.

High-performance organizations tend to put many things on a human scale — the size of plants, the size of work groups, and the units of work. How the company runs, where the people fit in, and how the work gets done are all comprehensible. People understand who or what influences their day-to-day activities. People understand where to go or whom to see when a problem arises. People understand on what basis they get paid. People simply understand.

Principle 10: People at the Top Know What Is Going On at the Bottom

People at the top in high-performance companies not only tend to gaze into crystal balls, but also to gaze at everyday operations. They are as concerned with the mundane daily activities as with the strategic issues of their company or industry.

There also seems to be a distinct lack of pretense or status in high-performance companies. In our present-day business environment, we have come to revere the chairman of the board, the CEO, and other top managers and to exalt them with golden parachutes because they are special. Within high-performance companies, everyone is special. The person at the bottom of the hierarchy has just as much to contribute, albeit in a different way, as the CEO. Top management people in high-performance companies understand this.

What does a CEO in a high-performance company do differently than CEOs in other companies? There has been much talk about vision and visioning, but not much talk about common or shared visions, having people be a part of what is going on. Individuals farther down the organization do not get slotted into the bright idea of the person at the top. They are not given the idea but are made part of the action and part of the idea. It is their idea.

Mark Pastin is particularly insightful when he states, "people will work harder, for less money, and above their abilities — if they are creating a new company." What the CEO does is create the enthusiasm (and, yes, sometimes even excitement) that is almost always present in high-performance companies. The common vision transforms an otherwise common job into something valuable.

Principle 10 is that people at the top know what's going on at the bottom. Perhaps a more accurate observation would be that people at the top care what is going on at the bottom. Sam Walton, chairman of Wal-Mart Stores, visits every one of his stores every year. Gary Comer, chairman of Lands' End, visits his operations many times each week. As a matter of fact, one Lands' End manager comments, "It seems that the larger we get the more often Gary is here." The scenarios may differ, but the actions at the top are always the same.

Caveats

The focal point of this chapter has been on the principles which appear to be central to high-performance operation. To use these principles effectively, though, several rules must be followed:

1. You must understand the basic paradoxes that exist. A common perception is that increased responsibility is the opposite of control. It is not.
2. You cannot pick and choose among the principles, selecting only those that you like. You have to take all of them, because they are all interrelated. It is the system that works, not the group of techniques. The techniques are a manifestation of the existing system.
3. There is no right way to implement the principles. Each company has to define the right way for its people, location, customers, and so forth. What is exactly right for one company may be exactly wrong for another company.

The value of the principles is that people become focused. People understand what has to be done. People understand who the real competitors are. It is not people or business units within the company, but those outside. And finally, people understand that they are not part of the organization but that they are the organization.

CHAPTER FOUR

Defining High Performance

Defining High Performance

Display is as false as it is costly.

— Benjamin Franklin

*T*HE preceding chapters provide an introduction, some
individual illustrations, and basic, underlying principles upon
which successful and productive companies operate. The focus
has emphasized the who, the what, and the where of companies
that achieve and maintain high levels of performance. This
chapter will focus on the why. Why, for example, do the
principles in the preceding chapter seem to work for some
companies, and why don't they appear to work in other
companies? Also, why will many of the programs being
implemented in companies around the United States today to
improve the effectiveness of organizational operations provide,
in the best cases, only short-term, positive results and, in the
worst cases, can even make the company worse off.

In general, the failures that do occur happen for quite predictable reasons. Probably the greatest cause of failure is ex-
pecting too much from too little. One concept or one program
is applied universally from one company to another company
with great expectations. And, the expectations are rarely, if
ever, met. The actual truth is that the expectations can't be met,
because high performance and high productivity will occur

only under certain conditions. Second, as with most evolving organisms, organizations change and develop over time and in response to their immediate surroundings. When programs are implemented, the existing level of organizational development is often not adequately taken into account. As a consequence, the attempts to improve productivity and effectiveness that are undertaken within many companies ultimately are viewed as being ill-conceived. The people involved in the process who are actually carrying out the programs inevitably become upset, frustrated, and, most unfortunately, discouraged with what is taking place.

The stories of failure heard on the corporate grapevine or read about in magazines and newspapers occurred because a great many of the programs put into operation promoted limited and sometimes singular outlooks. When that happens, what is carried out is quite different from what is anticipated, because individuals inevitably contribute only disappointing, half-hearted attempts. The news is not all bad, however, because nearly all of the information necessary for developing and maintaining high performance is already out there. But it is not always in the form that one might expect.

Developing High Performance

To understand high performance, one must first understand the activities that must take place for it to occur — the specific reasons or conditions that lead to sustained organizational success. The activities that have been shown to create high levels of performance are:

- Creating recognition
- Generating confidence
- Developing an individual-organizational fit
- Providing direction
- Building commitment

These activities generally aren't taught in school. Look in any management text. Rarely are any of these activities mentioned, much less discussed in any detail.

Recognition

In its most basic terms, for an organization to exist there have to be participants, people who are interested and willing to take part. To gain some measure of loyalty from these people, they must *become a part* of the organization. To gain high performance, people must not only become a part of, but also must belong to the organization. Furthermore, people have to *feel* that they belong to the organization. The way that we recognize people and make them feel that they belong is by paying attention to them.

Whether it's the person actually doing the job, the person's immediate superior, or an executive all the way at the top of the company, the most basic and useful activity that *any* employee can do is to pay attention. In fact, Tom Peters and Nancy Austin relate in *A Passion for Excellence* that attention is all there is. And, it is!

The problems that most companies are experiencing today come from a lack of attention. Probably it is more correctly stated that not enough attention is being given to the appropriate areas within the firm. Ron Brooks, a manager at Digital Electronics Corporation, relates: "The only thing we [managers] have is time. Where we put the time, in a way that is recognized, is what shows support and commitment."

From an organizational perspective, it is ironic that the one thing a manager is really paid to do generally isn't done well at all. Emphases are almost always placed on numbers. This observation is not meant to denigrate their importance, but it must be remembered that numbers are dead. They are historical and only report what has occurred, not what is happening.

Our regard for numbers is exacerbated by an almost excessive concern with the short term, not only in our corporations, but also in our personal lives (salary, promotions, and so forth). Numbers in the short term can always be manipulated. The real impact of ineffective operations can be and is quite easily disguised — at least for a time.

Why has our attention focused on numbers with a short-term emphasis? On a purely personal basis, what we pay attention to and how much attention we give is largely shaped by factors of which we are little aware. There are some compelling reasons for our individual perspectives. First, it comes from the culture. Not the corporate culture but the culture of our society, which affects people long before they ever get their first job. That culture says get ahead, be successful, it's the American way. Not that getting ahead and being successful are wrong, but it's the way that it is being done. Some people become too preoccupied with the fast track and, inevitably, become too busy looking up rather than looking around. To compound the problem, they are usually rewarded for knowing or being seen by the right people rather than for doing the right things. Most often though, it is just the daily routine. We fall prey to the traps that are set during a normal day — the paperwork, meetings, and commonplace crises that always seem to arise. It is easy to get sidetracked and not pay attention to whatever is not grabbing us by the throat.

If the desire is high performance, the first step has to be to instill a sense of belonging within *all* organizational members — every person. The way to create a sense of belonging is by recognizing individuals and treating them as if they are important to the organization. *Paying attention makes people feel worthwhile and* want to *contribute.* The word 'want' in the preceding sentence is perhaps the single most important factor in attainment of high performance.

Tom Peters and Nancy Austin were absolutely correct when they said attention is all there is. But they didn't go far enough. To paraphrase the late Vince Lombardi, hte late head coach of the world champion Green Bay Packers, attention isn't everything, it's the only thing.

Confidence

After attention is created and people feel they have worthwhile contributions to make, one more aspect is necessary to set the stage for rapidly achieving productive actions in the organization. This aspect is the generating of confidence among people within the organization. The magnitude of confidence prevailing within the organization is a direct function of the extent to which trust and credibility are being cultivated and the degree of integrity present in the actions being taken by people.

Implementing a climate or atmosphere of confidence requires that support and feedback be present in day-to-day interactions. These specific actions generate confidence because they augment and amplify the impact of the attention that is already being provided. Support and feedback, no matter where they come from, tell people that the attention they are getting is not phony and not a gimmick.

If we are paying attention and are concerned about a person and in what the person is doing, the only logical development is to allow the person to continue doing whatever is being done, as well as the person can. It makes no sense to pay attention and then not support the very thing you were supposedly concerned about. Support not only means providing help, it also means removing obstacles that can interfere with getting a job done. Details. Facts. Data. Knowledge. Wisdom. Assistance. Prompting. Resources. Advice. Encouragement. Guidance. Promoting. Each of these actions provides a point of support for an individual. In addition to support, we must also provide feedback. Feedback provides a knowledge of results, but it also involves information sharing about things related directly and indirectly to the job. Is there any kind of feedback that is not right? Basically no, but probably the best guideline that one can follow is that "employees can handle the negative feedback as long as they are working in an environment where they are respected, where they hear what they're doing right as well as what they're doing wrong, and where they have a chance to work and develop to their capacity."

When support and feedback are not provided, an organization is basically dooming itself to only mediocre productivity even in the best circumstances. If support is not given, one's ability does not ultimately determine success or failure. Instead, success or failure is determined by some outside cause. Circumstances can become frustrating and muddled as individuals start to perceive as contradictory the messages being sent by their superiors. When adequate feedback is not given, feelings of uncertainty and ambiguity are created within people. In addition, when feedback does occur, it is then often interpreted as threatening and fault-finding. If these feelings, caused by a lack of support and feedback, persist for any length of time, decreased effort results as people turn their energies into trying to make sure they don't do the wrong things rather than into trying to do the right things. Further, when support and feedback are lacking, it not only becomes a problem to get the job done right, sometimes it becomes a problem to get the job done at all!

Support and feedback create an openness in the organization. An openness to understand how what we and others are doing fits into the big picture. An openness that lets individuals believe in what others tell them. An openness to take action when things are not really clear. An openness to see and do new and better things.

Fit

Attention and trust form the nucleus for continuing high performance. To use an analogy, we might compare what is happening in the organization to a pump. Attention, credibility, integrity, and trust get people ready — or prime them, if you will.

The impact of increasing productivity becomes readily noticeable only when the people and the organization are fit together. It's not adjusting people to fit the organization as you would adjust a machine. Rather, fit is a mutual activity which considers and capitalizes upon the unique characteristics of each individual.

To make a person fit, he or she must first understand what the organization is all about, how it operates, and what is important to it. What we call corporate culture helps to do this. Corporate culture makes the operating environment comfortable and understandable for an individual.

But having a culture isn't enough. Corporate culture provides a foundation and a sense of stability. We also need a vision. Vision keeps things from being boring. Vision is seeing beyond what is there and what we are doing to what we can and should be doing. Vision is what adds excitement to what might otherwise be considered a mundane or routine job.

Until we can visualize what we want to occur or achieve, everything we do has the same meaning. Therefore, no priorities are set and people don't really care about what they do except to get it done. People assume roles as actors and actresses in the corporate play to get their paychecks so that they can do what they really want to do. What they do is generally something in which they can take personal pride. Another analogy will illustrate this point. A person who has a vision becomes like a child's toy that has been wound up tightly. The person can go in circles, can run into a wall, or can go into the direction that is best for the company. Providing vision is one of the manager's toughest jobs. It is tough because it requires translating what people at a higher level see and then putting into a form that can be understood and redesigned by subordinates into useful action.

Direction

With purpose comes motivation, but not necessarily productivity. In other words, we have a bunch of charged up people. So what do we do with them? We set them in the right direction. When they go in the right direction, they often surpass our wildest expectations. Exhibit 4.1 appropriately describes not what can happen, but what will happen.

Setting people in the right direction is initially accomplished through organizational focusing. Since every company has to produce something in the short-run or go out of business, there is an acute need to make sure that people do what the organization needs to have done — the necessary products or services. Organizations with highly-focused individuals are what we call (at least in the short-term) productive organizations. So, the more focused the activities of individual organizational members are, the more productive the organization becomes.

Setting people in the right direction is generally comprehensible in most organizations, since there is already a point of reference from which to start. The real problem becomes one of staying in the right direction. The corporate environment of today has been characterized as being dominated by change. Sometimes the change that is experienced is turbulent and sometimes the change is gradual. And we seem to always have organizations that are surprised in either event. There is always a bogeyman for them — the economy, the government, the unions, the Japanese, and so on.

Exhibit 4.1   *"Well, now, what have you two been doing all day?"*

Drawing by Chas. Addams; © 1986, The New Yorker Magazine, Inc.

The point is, change will come sometime from somewhere. Change is guaranteed. It will occur. The question is: Are we prepared to deal with the change? Focusing deals with what we have now, not what will be. So, while we are focusing, we also need to develop people. We create, in essence, new people in our organization, people who not only cope with threatening situations, but seize the opportunities that are there. As has been aptly pointed out by many, "Change creates opportunity." Only when we develop people to their full potential for our organization can we see change as the opportunity it really is and take advantage of it. More importantly, we experience true growth, not illusory growth, and get stronger instead of only bigger and fatter.

Commitment

The final activity is the development of commitment in the organization. An important distinction needs to be made about this stage. This is the distinction between commitment and loyalty. Commitment and loyalty are related, but not synonymous. Loyalty is almost always present when there is commitment, though the converse is not necessarily true. With loyalty, we do not necessarily get high performance and productivity. Only when we have commitment — real and tangible commitment — can the highest levels of quality, productivity, and innovation exist.

When people are committed, then quality, productivity, and innovation become common events. The impact of commitment can be seen in three distinct areas. First, people use their discretionary time, time that they could be using for other things, working for the organization. Why? Because they are motivated to do so, and they also receive satisfaction from doing their job and satisfaction from being associated with the organization. Their work life fits with their away-from-work life. It is not in competition with it. Second, typical organizational problems such as employee discipline or absenteeism are no longer problems that require major time and effort to resolve. We don't have to worry about dealing with grievances, hiring excess people, and so forth. In other words, the frequency of occurrence of disruptive and non-productive activities is minimized. Finally, the organization as a whole can be more creative. Because it is *their* organization, people will think about, and bring to the attention of their superiors, better ways of doing things. Conventional wisdom, for example, tells us that suggestion boxes don't provide much information for a company. Yet, if we examine Toyota we see that they can have a great impact. "In 1965, 39 percent of 9,000 employee suggestions (one per worker) were implemented; 15 tenacious years later, 94 percent of 859,000 suggestions (19 per worker) were approved." Unless we can generate a high level of commitment, conventional wisdom is totally correct about such things as the suggestion box.

To clarify the preceding discussion, the vast increase in productivity for a company comes as a function of: (1) people using their time better, (2) getting rid of non-productive activities, and (3) finding ways of doing current activities better. Until we reach this highest level in the model, an organization cannot ever hope to maximize productivity to its fullest extent.

Each of the activities has certain characteristic qualities associated with it. With commitment, what we accomplish is ownership which in turn is a function of individual and organizational persistence and consistency. This does not represent simple endurance or stamina but determination and perseverance, or what might be best described as relentless persistence. Organizations and the people in these organizations follow what they believe with tenacity. If it is not working, they fix it as best and as fast as they can.

A Model for High Performance

The preceding section provides a list of activities necessary for high performance. As you read through them, you probably recognized that a certain order was suggested. And you were correct. How you do the activities is just as important as what you do. Current research shows that the sequence needs to be taken into account to achieve maximum performance.

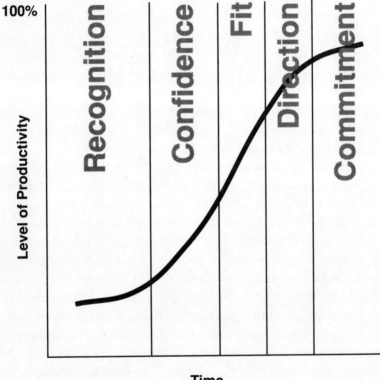

Figure 4.1   *Stages in the Development of High Performance*

The actual relationship among the different stages usually takes the appearance of Figure 4.1. Several key considerations are present in the relationship shown here. One must be aware of these considerations if high performance is to occur on a sustained basis. These considerations are:

1. A minimum threshold must be achieved before any perceptible effect takes place. When there is too little effort, little or no return is seen.
2. There are specific stages of development. Each stage has different implications for productivity and performance within an organization. *However, all stages are important.*
3. There is an ordered, sequential relationship among the stages. That is, an organization must in some way proceed through each of the particular stages in the process. Proceeding through each stage is important because every preceding stage provides the impetus for the development to the next stage. One cannot, for example, jump right into the middle of a process and realistically expect to be successful.

These three underlying considerations ultimately determine whether the program or group of programs adopted by a company will be successful, that is, achieve high levels of productivity. You must make sure the minimum investment is made, make sure your investment is made in the necessary things, and most importantly make sure you do the necessary things in the right order. Of the three points, "the ordered, sequential relationship" seems to present the most problems for today's businesses. Daniel Bills, chairman and president of Granville-Phillips Company, gives voice to this problem when he says, "It's not so much a question of which one of these [productivity] programs should you implement in your organization, it's a question of in what order should you implement all of them." When the Granville-Phillips Company initiated its productivity improvement programs, the company took whole programs "as is" from Japanese companies studied. As it turned out, the actions the company took worked. Daniel Bills observes, however, that "some actions were taken out of sequence by not realizing why they worked for the Japanese. We no longer make this type of mistake because now we have a very effective process for identifying root causes in a business environment."

There are several other practical observations about this particular model of organizational process. First, what we see in Figure 4.1 is that the initial stages of the model may not bring particularly high levels of productivity. But once the initial stages are attained, productivity increases tend to occur rather rapidly. Second, it is possible that more than one stage in the process of development can be worked on simultaneously. For example, if the atmosphere within the organization is not very negative, attention and credibility considerations can be dealt with at the same time. Likewise, fit and direction can sometimes be handled together effectively. Hence, an accurate current assessment is a fundamental requirement if constructive programs are to be developed. Last, one relevant and frequently asked question is: How long does it take a company to achieve high levels of productivity? The answer is that it depends. If the organization has maintained an atmosphere of conflict and adversarial relationships, then it may take a relatively long period of time. In general, actual practice and empirical research both seem to point to a typical range of about one to two years for developing significant degrees of organizational commitment and, therefore, a high level of individual performance.

The model presented in this chapter suggests that a certain

relationship exists between productivity and the particular stage of development of an organization. Within each stage of development, there needs to be a dominant individual focus. If the intensity of this individual focus is maintained, a certain organizational impact results. The association among the stages of development, organizational impact, and individual focus is summarized in Table 4.1.

Realities of High Performance

Using this model to develop high performance has two underlying realities associated with it. The first reality is that of achievement and the second reality is that of achieving. One

Ramifications of the Stages of Development		
Stage of development	**Organizational impact**	**Individual focus**
recognition	belonging	attention
confidence	trust integrity	support feedback
fit	purpose excitement	common vision shared vision
direction	insight	training development
commitment	ownership	persistence

Table 4.1   Ramifications of the Stages of Development

is concerned with getting there and the other is concerned with staying there. Both realities need to be understood if a company is not only to become successful, but also to remain successful.

The first aspect of this model, the reality of achievement, is the reality of the self-fulfilling prophecy. If we think people can't or won't do what they're supposed to do, then they won't. If we think people can do what they should and we support their actions, they will. It is that simple. At this point, someone is undoubtedly thinking, "There are no controls, and that's stupid." The controls may look different than those we are traditionally used to seeing, but they certainly are present. The function of a control is to make sure that everything is operating smoothly and correctly. Controls do not necessarily have to be threatening and stifle people to prove that they are functioning properly. As we progress through the different stages of development, each new stage creates new types of control. In the end, we have control from the top, from our peers, and from below.

The model also points out the reality of achieving. In a sense, there is never really the attainment of 'The Goal,' only a striving to attain the goal in its new form. What this means is that once we have accomplished what we originally set out to do, we are not finished. It is a continuing process. As the business environment and competition change, or as our own organization and its people change, it is easy to fall prey to the very same adversity or distress that we may have conquered at an earlier time. Reaching the top may be difficult, but staying at the top is far more demanding because we do not become immune to any of the problems we mastered earlier. The reality of achieving is the reality of being relentless. While organizations or individuals need not and perhaps should not be obsessive, they must exhibit relentless persistence to maintain the qualities that created the success in the first place. Once we have attained high levels of productivity, it becomes easy to rationalize not doing some of the things that enabled us to get where we are. The unfortunate consequence is that we fall prey to adversities that we initially faced head on — and beat.

CHAPTER FIVE

Finding the Yellow Brick Road

Finding the Yellow Brick Road

We judge ourselves by what we feel capable of doing.
Others judge us by what we've already done.
— Henry Wadsworth Longfellow

O NE of the points brought out in the preceding chapter is that in attempting to develop high performance there is a minimum investment that must be made. The perception might exist that it would be fairly easy to attain the minimum investment as long as we are vigilant. This is an erroneous perception. The fact is, it will be quite difficult for many organizations.

The difficulty exists because there are two main hurdles that generally remain unrecognized as barriers to organizational effectiveness. One of the hurdles affects all organizations, and the other hurdle, while it is not common to all organizations, troubles quite a few in one form or another. This double hurdle makes attaining the first stage anything but easy.

Alienation, the first hurdle we face, arises from the legacy of our modern mass-consumption society and the massive mechanized industries it has spawned. Reflective of this circumstance, one study reports that "22 percent of them [people in organizations] mistrust management and 43 percent hold such jaundiced views of the world that they are generally suspicious of other people, including their fellow workers." Thus, even if we are the most enlightened of companies and are eager for high performance, the sad truth is that a fair amount, if not most, of the people within any organization start out with a negative perspective. If the people with negative perspectives happen to be managers, the programs they implement will be doomed from their inception. Two Canadian researchers, Manfred Kets de Vries and Danny Miller, point out that when people enter an organization they generally start out with low or negative satisfactions for both the organization and their job. Satisfaction does increase. The increase in satisfaction is only illusory, though, because it arises from the fact that the individual "begins to more fully appreciate the realities of organizational life and to understand the limitations of his or her job." They go on further to state, "One learns what to expect from the organization or one lowers one's expectations." Not a very heartening observation.

The same two researchers also point out what I would classify as a second significant hurdle: Organizations, much in the same fashion as an individual, can be neurotic. These neurotic organizations exhibit the same classical dysfunctional behaviors, fantasies, and associated dangers as have been reported for people. Needless to say when neurotic organizations interact with negative individuals, we have a double-barreled problem that creates some powerful negative barriers.

The net result is that people have come to expect that they will not be fully included in their organization, will not have their particular abilities utilized, and in general, have come to mistrust almost any actions that are taken — ironically even those that may be beneficial. Everybody needs and seeks a sense of belonging. If we listen to people, we discover: (1) they belong to a family and are usually proud of its members; (2)

they belong to some group or club and are proud of the association; and (3) many have a hobby of which they are proud. These people spend many and sometimes long hours at something for which they are paid little or nothing. If we listen to them talk, they get very animated and excited about what they are doing.

Why can't they belong to the place they work? We spend half or more of our waking hours during the average week doing our jobs. Yet, only a relatively few of us feel any sense of real belonging to our companies.

How do you make people feel like they belong? There is no universal formula. There are many means to the same end. The proper course of action depends upon the person, the job, and the environment of the company itself. The common denominator in all situations is recognizing people as individuals. The plain and uncomplicated act of paying attention counteracts the systematic exclusion and ignoring of people that has become commonplace in our complex society.

Where It All Begins

Does paying attention sound simple? It is. Does it sound too simple? Well, it isn't.

There are two kinds of attention. One relates to the person and the other relates to the activities that the person is doing. At the most basic level, there needs to be a concern for people just for themselves. A sense and a realization that all individuals are worthwhile and are contributing has to be nurtured. This kind of attention leads not only to an increase in an individual's self-esteem but also to an increase in an individual's overall activity and perception. People who have self-esteem do more and better things. The person who feels valued will do extra things, the little things that always make a difference (in dollars) for the organization when they are added up.

While making a person feel good is important, it doesn't necessarily pay the bills. Attention also has to be paid to what people do. Putting attention into action so that it not only makes a person feel good but leads to the fulfilling of organizational objectives is certainly one of the strong points at ServiceMaster. One example of how ServiceMaster provides attention is through the positive incident reports that are commonly used. When somebody goes beyond their job description, they are "written-up." Ken Fisher, director for people development, relates: "Suppose a groundskeeper spots some people who have been locked out of a meeting, gets off his tractor and lets them into the building. That's an opportunity for the supervisor to build self-esteem by writing a positive incident report and giving a copy of it to the groundskeeper, who can take it home and show it to his or her family." If a superior is concerned about a subordinate's work, then the subordinate will care about his or her work. If a superior is marginally concerned about what a subordinate is doing, then the subordinate will care only marginally about the work. If a superior is not concerned about the subordinate's work, then the subordinate will not care either. These simple psychological principles provide profound results when put into action.

The work itself has to be seen as being valuable rather than as being just another activity. Organizational researcher Judi Komacki notes in her examination of successful and unsuccessful managers that it is not just how much attention a person receives but also the kind of attention that is given. In particular, her findings point out that successful managers tend to do two things: gather data on performance by actually viewing what is going on and transmit their knowledge of the performance levels to their subordinates. One of her more interesting findings is that contrary to what most managers think, relatively little time is spent in these particular types of activities, whether the manager is successful or not. It amounts to only about 10 percent of all managerial time spent, regardless of the level within the organization. In summarizing her findings, she cleverly asserts, "You get what you _inspect_, not what you _expect_."

Although as managers, we need to be concerned about what people are doing, we must also appreciate that we have to "give the people space to be recognized for their own initiative rather than for doing it [our] way. What we want to do in the workplace is facilitate commitment to doing a good job." To get the right things done, the ultimate realization within any organization is that _the managing work is no more important (or even really any different for that matter) than the doing work._

While attention can only be created at the individual level, a vital realization should be that the organization itself can have a significant impact on the amount and frequency of attention present. Attention from a superior to a subordinate is of foremost importance, but all of the really powerful organizations have built-in mechanisms so that individuals consistently develop a recognition of each other. When attention is solely an individual phenomenon (that is, superior to subordinate) there can be an unevenness. People have busy days, people have days they are ill, and people have emotional days when they just don't feel like attending to others.

When attention is built into the system, however, this unevenness tends to be smoothed out. How do you build it into the system? Many techniques have been used. It could be part of a bonus system, it could come from an immediate work group, it could be a luncheon recognizing people for doing the right things, it could be part of a communication system, or it could be part of a corporate education system. High performing companies usually employ some or all of the previous techniques. Individual attention is magnified and reinforced by an overall system. The key point is that attention is paid to the individual and his or her work, no matter how far down the individual is on the ladder of the organization. Each person and what the person does are seen as being valuable. This is not just hoopla, as some see it, but only recognition of what is already there!

Given that attention is necessary, is there a right way to do it? Management By Walking Around? Being a One-Minute Manager? Yes, both of those ways are right, and there are many other right ways too. Several studies exemplify what attention is and how it can be achieved. One study reports that treating people with respect, having confidence in their abilities, and providing self-esteem are notable methods. Another study points out that giving credit for ideas, the way one is treated when a mistake is made, following through to get problems solved, consistency in behavior, and listening when something of perceived importance is said are significant. Still another study relates that feedback which includes what was done well, allowing people to interact during discussion (not cutting them off), expressing greetings upon meeting and departing, and even just maintaining eye contact are all meaningful actions. Each study reports what appears to be different views and opinions, but what becomes evident in the diversity of responses is that all of the studies seem to reach a single focal point. Any technique can be right and any technique can be wrong. It just depends on how it is being used.

For example, one popular technique, Management By Walking Around (MBWA) that consists of just walking around and being seen but not really paying attention, is worthless except as physical exercise. But, if whatever you do makes people feel like they're part of the organization and that they belong, then it is the right kind of attention. As a general statement, the right kind of attention is anything that allows individuals to feel that the organization in which they work is THEIR organization.

Everybody coming into an organization feels that they have some special ability or talent. Only by paying attention can we ever find out what people think is special about themselves. When people's special abilities are overlooked, they become frustrated and even mad. When people are overlooked enough times they become alienated. This creates or reinforces previously held negative perceptions of the organization. A remark such as "People around here don't care who you are or what you can do" is not just a sign of individual frustration, but really a signal of a more widespread organizational productivity problem. Why do people take extra sick days, miss work, leave early, or cause disciplinary problems? Right, they feel that nobody cares. And they're right. Except about the numbers, nobody does care.

Attention is the first, most basic, and absolutely necessary step in transforming a company from a group of people into an organization. Opportunities must be created for people to interact in ways that are not simply "my job" to "your job." Hence, attention needs to occur in a variety of ways. It can be spontaneous or planned. It can be at work or away from work. It can be something complex or it can be something as simple as just saying hello to someone. Or, it can take the form of regard for the person or the job that person happens to be doing. The potency of attention is greatest when attention comes not only from superior to subordinate, but from peer to peer and from people at the top to people at the bottom and vice versa. The rules for paying attention aren't very complicated except that the attention can't be:

- contrived,
- artificial, or
- insincere.

If it is any of the above, then it is not paying attention and whatever you are doing is wasting your time and the other person's time, too.

Generating Confidence

Once we are paying attention, people must not feel that what has already taken place is a fluke, trick, or manipulation. The attention that is provided to people within the organization sets the stage for what is to come and escalates individual anticipations and expectations. After the initial recognition stage, we need to generate a feeling of confidence by creating an environment where trust can exist. People don't trust other people that they don't know. Without recognition, there can be no trust.

How do you build trust with others? Simply by making promises and keeping them. That's it.

The easy response is that we can't be responsible for our business environment or the constantly changing general economy. While this is true, the real challenge for managers is to discriminate between those promises that we can really keep and those that we offer to make someone feel good or to get someone off our back when we are busy. The first place to look is in the past to see what we have been able to do and what things we have failed to do. And while we can't fulfill every promise, the simple act of discriminating those that we can definitely do from those that we probably can't do will go a long way toward creating a more positive environment.

A close companion to trust is integrity. Many people tend to put integrity on a relatively high moral plane and thereby discount what it means for an organization or themselves individually. Integrity is, in fact, not very complex at all. Peter Block provides one of the best and most practical definitions of what integrity is. He describes integrity as simply:

...to put into words what we see happening, to tell people what is really going on within our unit and what we see going on outside our unit. Integrity isn't a moral issue; it's not a question of fraud or legally dishonest acts. It is more the issue of whether it is possible for us to tell the truth about what we see happening, to make only those promises that we can deliver on, to admit our mistakes, and to have the feeling that the authentic act is always best for the business.

Tell it like it is. Don't commit to things that can't be produced. When things go wrong, don't deny it or blame someone else. Keep people informed. These are actions of integrity. Integrity is common sense and respect for the other person. But most of all, it frees us from some of the burdens that we don't have to carry and we shouldn't carry. It allows us to focus on what we're doing rather than on the periphery. Buck Rogers elaborates on integrity by relating that "The hardest thing for most managers is telling someone he's not performing well. But you owe it to people to be honest. First, you need to determine if it's a personal problem or a business problem. You ask the why, not just dictate. Anybody can be autocratic. But you don't get much done that way, through fear. A good manager leads through his or her own honesty and integrity."

Where does integrity begin? If we accept the preceding description, then it can begin anywhere. All persons can act with integrity within their sphere of activities. It is obviously best if integrity runs throughout the organization, but anyone can exhibit integrity, and it doesn't necessarily have to affect the individual's career negatively.

The memo and the notes scrawled on the memo in Exhibit 5.1 illustrate the value one major corporation places on integrity. The memo was sent by John Pepper, then CEO of Procter & Gamble. Aside from the memo itself, which provides a

CC-DMT   cc to each:

"Nuf Said" JAS

KB 3/6

February 25, 1986

SUBJECT: SOMETHING WE MUST LIVE BY....ALWAYS

We must maintain and build a culture and environment where honesty and
integrity are the most valued characteristics of all. Where people say what
they think is right, not what they think other people want to hear. Where
there is a full understanding that realistic answers are all that are wanted
and that there is no belief, deeply felt and honestly put, that won't be
considered with an open mind.

and that DISAGReement even held positions ARE NeveR A CAReer-limiting FACTOR. Job performance determines JEP:cl CAReeRS -- Not 5924p whether your Judgment disagreed with the boss on AN issue.

This is the ultimate "K.Is of Death" which I've seen kill several promising CAReeRS. Aside from JEP's integrity Issue, there ARE other pragmatic factors: ① No ORGANIZATION.. small or Large-- will follow a "Leader" who shows this characteristic -- AND it always shows. ② Nobody can pull this off successfully for very L you can't read the other guy's mind that sooner or Later you're discovered.

Exhibit 5.1   Memo

strong message, the comments of the recipients, who are managers further down the line, are also worthy of consideration. Comments such as: "This (telling other people what they want to hear) is a kiss of death which I've seen kill several promising careers," or "No organization — small or large — will follow a 'leader' who shows this characteristic — and it always shows," or "Nobody can pull this off successfully for very long. You can't read the other guy's mind that well; sooner or later you're discovered." All quite interesting perceptions of what happens when integrity is not present. The fact that comments were even made represents an affirmation not of the person at the top who sent the memo, but an acknowledgment of the values that are already in place within the organization.

In order to develop trust and integrity, one must make support and feedback something that becomes second nature in interactions with others. An initial tendency might be to read what has been said so far as meaning to provide better communication. It is not simply better communication, though communication is an integral part. What it means is the quality, the intangible aspect, of the communication. It is actively providing people with information that is relevant to what they are doing.

Wittingly or unwittingly, we often hoard information. We make judgments. We try to determine whether somebody really needs to know certain things. What are the results of this? Others have the perception of something being hidden or perhaps the perception that certain people are not smart enough or valuable enough to have what we possess. Unfortunately, sometimes these are not false perceptions on the part of other people but are the actual beliefs of the person who has the information. Most companies that have adopted a free flow of communication have determined that the cost-benefit relationship of doing this lies far in the favor of benefit for the organization.

To provide support and feedback, the first step must start with listening (really listening to what people are saying) so that you can understand and properly provide what people need. Your subordinates are just as much your customers as are the people who buy your product or service. They are internal customers providing the means to create the product or service for the external customers.

A climate of confidence means more than simply sharing information. Even though sharing information generally creates significant benefits, it is in reality only a small part of this stage. We have to go beyond what are really little more than passive actions and actively provide support for what people are doing, helping them to do a better job.

Much of the time when a subordinate does a bad job it's the superior's fault because of a lack of support. Support represents a connectedness from the top of an organization to the bottom. Support is the realization that we are all on the same team. Support is understanding that to be successful as individuals (that means everyone in the organization) we have to be successful as a group.

Life is competition. From our own limited individual perspectives, it is easy to interpret this as meaning competing against others for promotions, raises, and so forth. Too many times jobs are seen as adversarial activities within an organization rather than as joint efforts. We become completely blind to who our real competitors are. When support and feedback are present, the immediate work environment is transformed from a threatening experience into one that is encouraging and maybe even enjoyable.

Within an organization, trust and integrity become intertwined to form what might be generally described as credibility. In the organizational frame of reference, credibility takes on a complex character in that it is a combination of trustworthiness, perceived competence, and vitality. This mixture of good judgment, skill, dependability, and being actively concerned about people creates a sense of vigor and well-being.

Some companies have policy manuals that are nearly a foot thick to guide behavior and others have their principles written on one sheet. What is the difference? Trust. Integrity. Credibility.

Management experts Frank Kuzmits and Lyle Sussman point out that there are two reasons why any manager should be concerned about credibility. "First, if you have credibility, you can make an occasional mistake and not worry about being perfect. Your employees will compensate for your imperfections because they know that deep down you have their best interests at heart." This first reason is certainly worthwhile, but the second reason is perhaps more meaningful in that it may be the most potent means of persuasion available to an individual manager. They elaborate on the importance of this second reason by saying that "credibility can be acquired and enhanced. In other words, this powerful management tool does not have the elusive aura of charisma. Any person who wants to be a better manager can do so by acquiring credibility, enhancing the credibility he possesses or making sure that his credibility is not diminished."

The person who uses his or her ability and energy to turn words into action is a person who accumulates much credibility from both above and below. Furthermore, as we create credibility, we formulate a track record that generates a confidence that things will continue — and even get better.

One Manager's Story

This is the account of a manager in the manufacturing operation of a large multinational company. This manager took over a department that basically had old equipment and high costs. There were seven other "competitor departments" producing the same product within the organization. This department was dead last in the cost competition to produce the product — eighth out of eight.

By the time the manager was moved to her next position, less than one year later, the department had moved up from the bottom to the fourth position on an annual costs basis. Further, during many of the months, the department even enjoyed the second and third cost position for that month. Only one department consistently out-produced this particular depart-ment, and it was the newest department, with high technology equipment.

What did this manager do to turn around productivity? First, she went out to where the action was. Not that this particular action was striking, but a number of her predecessors rarely did it. They were managers, you see. At first, she just watched what the people in her department were doing and talked about the operations. She didn't meddle with what the supervisors were doing. She was just concerned about what was going on and what people were doing. One of the first actions she deemed important was to keep the machines running through lunch. When the mechanics wouldn't help the operators, instead of putting her supervisors in the middle, she simply went out and kept them running herself.

Then she did something that none of her immediate predecessors had done. She posted the semi-monthly cost results for all the different departments around the country. Was she breaking company rules in doing this? No. Her predecessors just thought that this kind of information was management information and so didn't see fit to share it. The philosophy of "What they don't know won't hurt them" was a guiding rule and they were right. It didn't hurt the workers, not nearly as much as it hurt the managers themselves and the company as the productivity and profits from the department languished.

Most of what happened is rather simple. Did she do anything else that was responsible for her results? Yes, she took a page right out of a management textbook. When people started doing good things, things that made the department run better, she gave them a sticker. Yes, a sticker just like the ones that kids collect. Except these were adults whose ages ranged from their mid-thirties to mid-fifties. Some stickers had a message; others didn't. One of the most unexpected aspects during this turn around was that the person who was tabbed as the troublemaker of the department also proudly displayed his stickers on his locker. Somehow the work became fun. Same jobs, same people. What happened? What was different? Someone was now concerned with what was going on and someone was concerned with being productive. The people not only did a better job, but had fun doing it. People were shown that they made a difference on a daily basis with the stickers, and people were shown that they made a difference overall when the semi-monthly results were posted.

Arguably the biggest irony is that about half-way through her tenure as manager in the department, it was announced that the department would be closed down because of past inefficiencies. What do you think happened? Nothing. The people continued to work just as hard as before even knowing that their department would be closed. One doesn't have to think very hard to realize what might have happened if the department hadn't been shut down and the manager had been allowed to continue. Perhaps the most interesting question of all was: What message was being passed on? Not just to the people in the department but to others in the plant? In other plants? Does hard work pay off? Was the company really interested in productivity? You answer the questions.

Actions and Reactions

We have come to the realization that our organizations are not as productive as they should be only because we have been forced to see that somebody else is doing it better. Whose fault is it? One frequent perception is that people don't work as hard as they used to work. Comments such as "They're lazy" and "They don't care" are also made regularly. Other people, mainly top management, throw up their hands in disgust.

These perceptions and comments are right and they are wrong. Based on its research, the Public Agenda Foundation has observed, "Although work behaviors are indeed deteriorating, there is still a broadly shared endorsement of the work ethic in all sectors of the American workforce." The report concludes, "The conventional wisdom of a deteriorating work ethic is badly off-target; the American work ethic is strong and healthy, and may even be growing stronger." Perhaps the observation of E. J. Cattabiani, executive vice-president of Westinghouse, capsulizes why much of the decrease in productivity we have experienced has taken place: "Good people do not mind hard work. They thrive on it. What they mind is work that goes unrecognized...or ideas that can't penetrate layers of middle managers who feel the need to be smarter than the people they monitor."

An apparent contradiction develops as we try to put an organization on the road to high performance. The contradiction is that only toward the end of the second stage do we really see significant increases in performance, which leads to the perception that little is happening for the investments that are being made. The reason, in some cases, that it takes so long is that the primary function of the initial stages is to lay groundwork for what is to come. The first two stages attempt to overcome the alienation and other negative individual perspectives that are present. The observation has been made that

"The lack of trust has been found to be more negative in its effect than presence of trust is positive in its influence — in other words, it is more damaging not to trust than it is helpful to trust." Developing credibility, just like developing recognition in the first stage, makes up for the deficiencies that exist, and the true impact doesn't really become observable until later.

The above observations are organizational problems, but what is of the most significance is that they can be attacked by individuals. The means of attack are attention, support, and feedback. These three actions are undoubtedly the most powerful actions any manager can take. Why? Simply because these actions can be done by anyone, anywhere, and at anytime. As we progress to higher levels of performance, much comes to depend primarily upon the organization. However, as was mentioned earlier, the first two stages do not necessarily require input from the organization. It doesn't matter whether you work for a good organization, a mediocre organization, or even a poor organization. In other words, any manager can almost always make things better in his or her immediate operating arena by adopting the three captivating actions — attention, support, and feedback. Conversely, when things aren't going as well as desired, the manager should also examine whether any of the three are missing.

CHAPTER SIX

Creating Your Destiny

CHAPTER SIX

Creating Your Destiny

The obstacle that most often stands in the way of progress is not ignorance but the illusion of knowledge.
— Duncan B. Sutherland, Jr.

*T*HE principal functions of the first two stages are to remove negative expectations and to establish initial orientations for people in the organization. What we develop during this time is, at best, a loose relationship, but one where a person understands what the organization wants and also one where a person can rely on the people with whom he or she has to interact. What does not exist is the level of productivity that can come only when individuals are integrated into an organization's activities. Starting from this point in an organization's growth, the degree of individual integration (and, not so incidentally, productivity) escalates quite rapidly as greater levels of maturity are achieved.

Because of required levels of trust and credibility, only as we arrive at the midpoint of development can we actively start to fit the person and the organization together. It is at this point that a bridge is formed between individual and organizational perspectives. The way this fit is created is through the organizational vision. Corporations today are so large and have so many different stakeholders in their operations that it is often quite difficult to articulate a vision, let alone assemble one that is understandable to everyone. In most instances, even when an overall corporate vision is created, individuals are typically left up to their own devices to figure out how and if they fit into where they think the organization is going.

Where We Arrive Depends Upon Where We Are Going

The vision of an organization needs to be both abstract and concrete. It declares values that we think are important and the circumstances we desire to advance and encourage. It also provides an image of the kind of organization we wish to create and in what direction we wish the organization to go. "Vision is a crystallization of what you want to create. Vision takes your generalized desire and shapes it into a clear and definable result." Why vision leads to productivity is shown in its organizational impact. When vision is a dominant force in a company's operations, the organizational impact emerges as purpose and excitement within individuals.

Having a vision is having a purpose. Vision creates a focal point, which in turn creates the driving force within each person. When people have a purpose, they work hard because they are accomplishing something that's worthwhile and meaningful to them. That is exactly why the people at Delta Airlines gave back $30 million to buy a jet for the company. The jet was a tangible manifestation of the company's vision. The second impact, excitement, while not often discussed, should not be overlooked as a meaningful consequence of a vision. Only when vision exists, can we transform the ordinary and make something different out of routine sameness. We've seen and may even have known people who were excited about their company and what was happening in it. Yet, other people in companies in the same business with similar technology do not have the same excitement. Why?

Where there is excitement and enthusiasm there also is usually some kind of vision. People don't get excited about jobs,
they get excited about possibilities. Vision is the articulation
of possibilities.

Only when a person fits in the organization as an actual part
of the operations rather than just a performer of operations
does it makes sense to that person to use discretionary time, at
work and away, to do organizational activities better. That
person no longer defines his or her relationship with the
company just in terms of a "job." The key point in the preceding discussion, though, is the use of discretionary time. With
this kind of thinking, traditional measures of productivity
become largely inadequate. We use machine capacity, facility
utilization, inventory turnover, and the like as our measures
of how productive we are. What we in general don't consider
is how people use (or don't use, as the case may be) their time
to make the organization more productive.

Lincoln Electric, one of the companies presented in Chapter
2, exhibits what productivity means in the really productive
company. Lincoln received steel sheets from a supplier for use
in its operations. When problems started to arise, the situation
was examined. The result was that Lincoln did something it
had never done before. It purchased the steel in rolls, purchased a machine to process the rolled steel (which paid itself
off in six months, by the way), and provided the steel in the
form necessary for its operations.

The responses "It's obvious" and "No big deal" might be
made. The point is, it is obvious and indeed even expected at
Lincoln, but it just doesn't happen, at least not very often, at
other companies. Why did this happen at Lincoln and why
does it rarely happen in other organizations? The answer is,
discretionary time. In most companies, only certain people
think about the organization, and most of the time it is usually

during working hours. People turn themselves on and off. At Lincoln Electric, people don't just try to do their job better, they try to make their organization better. In the truly productive companies, almost all people think about making their organization better — using their discretionary time. Since most of a person's time, even while at work, is discretionary, when we disregard this component in the productivity equation we are, in essence, giving up control over most of our productivity.

Earlier in the book, the relevance of corporate purpose was discussed, but just as relevant are individual purpose and the excitement that goes along with it. So it should go without any further discussion that the most critical aspect of vision is personalizing it. Making the vision a personal statement for each individual is what makes a vision a vision rather than a dream. This is not just enrolling someone else in your vision, but making it come alive for them.

To be successful, an organizational vision needs to be a common vision and a shared vision. The vision means more than having everyone understand what someone at the top wants. It is having each individual *want* to achieve the vision. It might start out as an idea from someone at the top but it is not something handed down as an edict. It is something that takes shape; that is, becomes real and more defined with each person's input. Each person's thumbprint, no matter how small, is indelibly etched into the vision.

Why a vision creates purpose and excitement is that it allows individuals to create their own organization. Individuals have a hand in creating what goes on around them. In a very real sense, they have a hand in shaping their own destiny. Where there is no vision, the perception of the world becomes one where people get fired, are told what to do and how to do it. Everything is beyond an individual's control. Since people use their discretionary time only on those things they can control, an important part of any manager's role is to work with subordinates to help them perceive and articulate their own personal vision of greatness for the future. Creating a vision is not to have others embrace _our_ vision but to support others in embodying their vision.

Sight Beyond Sight

One of the biggest misconceptions and, therefore, one of the biggest stumbling blocks, about creating a vision is that it has to be highly creative or imaginative. Creativity and imagination are certainly involved, though nothing beyond the capabilities of almost anyone. The indispensable part of creating a vision isn't even concerned with creativity.

The initial step in trying to formulate a vision requires us to become aware of and understand that what is confronting us is reality. In his Emmy Award-winning series on creativity, Bill Moyers presents one definition of imagination as simply being the ability to see what is there. It sounds almost too elementary. But many people either do not see what is there or else deny what exists.

Robert Fritz presents several reasons why many choose not to see what is actually there: "One reason...is that current reality might make you look bad. Another reason is that it might make others look bad, and you feel the need to protect them. Thirdly, current reality might be threatening because you `should not' be where you actually are." Whether it is these specific reasons or others really doesn't matter, because, as Fritz persuasively observes, "What is actually occurring in current reality occurs independently of our perception of it. Current reality does not disappear just because it may go unrecognized." The unfortunate result of stumbling on this first step, he notes, is that "every year thousands of businesses go bankrupt slowly and inconspicuously as the people in those organizations hide current reality from each other in an attempt to 'look good.'"

Once we accept reality, the creation of a vision is easy because we are starting from somewhere and starting with accurate information. Once the cobwebs are cleared away, we can think about what we really want to do. As we move down the organization, our grand vision gets translated and refined into the grand visions of the rest of the people in the organization. Although the impetus for the vision starts at the top, the vision at the top and the vision at the bottom of the organization should really be the same because of the interaction and modification that take place in the process.

We now come to the part where people seem to have the most difficulty — the so-called creative part. What happens almost miraculously, though, after we articulate current reality, is that the creative part is not so difficult after all. It might even be easy. We find out that revealing the truth about current conditions is the demanding part. The creative part appears to be difficult only because what we are looking at is not clear. Creating a vision without clarity is like trying to look out of a dirty window.

Once we are actively creating the vision, we need to be alert to two dangers. The first danger is what might be called the "Camelot phenomenon." This occurs when we produce a vision that is exciting, but so quixotic that people inevitably become disappointed and then disenchanted. The inescapable result will be skepticism and a large step backward as credibility is lost. A second danger is having a vision that is not one vision. This occurs when there are "so many visions that employees drown in the confusion." Not only do individuals within the organization become puzzled about where they are going, but also about what the company wants. In addition to individual confusion, the organization as a whole becomes muddled in both its thinking and actions. It is not just the future that is in jeopardy, however, because "companies who create and communicate annual _re_visions are likely to find themselves ignoring the present." When we do this, we lose what is to come, and we lose the here and now.

Creating a vision creates impetus for an organization. While it is not an easy task, it is not an impossible one. What we are confronted with is not the difficulty of being creative, but the difficulty of accurately understanding the existing circumstances. This is the exact meaning Bill Moyers was trying to get across when he described imagination as the ability to see what is there. In creating our vision, we need to make sure it is a common vision and a shared vision so that we do not end up with something that is unrealistic or confusing. Creating a vision is not enough, though. The vital part for a company is that everybody _lives_ the vision.

Fueling the Fire

Once we have people fit into the organization or, more properly, create conditions where people feel that they are the organization as opposed to working for the organization, we can assist them in setting up the right direction for now and in the future. Since the inertia (which also can be read as motivation) already exists, what we attempt to do is maximize individual output.

At this juncture of development, the concern is with making today better, with an even greater concern for making sure there will be a tomorrow — an even better tomorrow. At this point, we try to fashion the enthusiasm and excitement previously generated into organizational terms and channel it back into the specific tasks that have to be accomplished to create quality products and services for our customers. The difference now is that the tasks, although they still may be the same, are seen in a different light. So in reality, the tasks or jobs really are different because they carry a new and different meaning. While we are concerned with the current activities, we are equally or more concerned with what will be happening. Probably the best practical application of what should be going on is illustrated by the activities taking place within ServiceMaster. The process at ServiceMaster emphasizes the development of people within its organization. In simple terms, they help people to *do* and to *be*. It should be noted that the development of people is not abstract but is done within the context of ServiceMaster's culture, its customers' needs, and the services it provides.

One part of this stage is concerned with doing — the now of our business, how the company helps its people to do a better job currently. If technical expertise is involved, it is provided. If the industry has rapidly changing technology, the company updates skills or knowledge. The bottom line is that people can do the best job. In addition to skill development, individuals are taught corporate values. If, for example, we view Motorola, we see the company's commitment to education with an advanced learning center at the corporate headquarters and a satellite network to many Motorola plants. What is more prominent are the offerings provided. The course catalog is an undertaking worthy of a university. It lists and describes courses and relates them to career tracks (an illustration of which was provided in Chapter 3). In addition to learning technical and managerial skills, people can take courses related to corporate values such as quality, dealing with customers, or a basic component of the organization itself — the Participative Management Process. The doing portion, which should include everyone, has many facets which need to be treated in a systematic fashion. The doing portion should include knowledge and an understanding of what is going on and why.

As was stated earlier, in addition to proper training of employees, "new" people are needed within the organization to deal with eventualities that cannot now be envisioned. The only choices available are to acquire more people with the necessary new skills and perspectives, or develop the people who are already part of the company into the new people that are needed. Many companies have taken the first path and these same companies generally end up having excess people and fluctuating productivities. Fewer companies have taken the second path and have chosen to develop the people they have into the people they need. To avoid the cyclical purging that usually takes place, along with its negative repercussions, and to ensure a more critical competitive posture in our current business environment, the second path provides the best insurance and really the only way. In ServiceMaster terms, while we are helping people to do, we also have to help them to be. We have to help them to develop latent abilities. While this sounds a bit altruistic — and it can be altruistic — it is also a business necessity. We have to help people in the organization to be more than they are now, because the company and its competitive environment will be more than it is now. Unlike machinery, people do not depreciate. The choice is to waste past investments or take an asset with a known value and create a greater value.

So far, providing direction has been presented rather one-dimensionally, that is, in relatively formal terms. Formal training and development needs to be reinforced and put into perspective or given a meaning in the day-to-day activities of the organization. Coaching and mentoring provide the "personal tutoring" for understanding classroom, workshop, or seminar training. Skills and knowledge are given a richness and dimension that can never be achieved solely within a formal setting. In fact, formal training and development without coaching and mentoring fall far short of the results they should produce. But to be successful, this highly personal process must be an ongoing and continuous activity. Based on the results of his research, Jerry Willbur reflects that "it would be tempting to speculate that a manager must always be mentored first to learn to give quality mentoring to a protege´." He further presents the following business implications:

- Both mentors and protege´s definitely benefit from mentoring.
- Corporate training programs should include courses on how to give mentoring, as well as programs on how to get mentored.
- Corporations should look at the educational levels demanded for success at each career stage, and find ways to provide this important success predictor.

Learning should be an active rather than a passive occurrence within an organization. Learning should be a widely, rather than narrowly-defined event. When learning is active, research shows, necessary changes can be implemented far more quickly than would take place by natural occurrence. As an organization continues to mature, we see significant, and perhaps new, investments being required of the organization. These investments made by the organization are more than matched, however, by the potential available for increased productivity. The commitment to learning is not just an investment in being better prepared for future eventualities, but it is also tangible proof to everyone in the organization that the company is making an investment in itself.

Achieving the Pinnacle

In the final stage, the stage of commitment, what comes into existence is a sense of ownership. This is not ownership according to any legal definition but ownership that comes from creating and controlling what goes on and a belief in the process of the organization (See Table 6.1. In one sense, this last stage is only a culmination of what has preceded. Without question, it is a realization that comes from the consistency and persistence that is exhibited by people throughout the organization.

To examine this stage, we first need to understand what commitment is. Commitment is not a dichotomy, that is, something you have or don't have. Rather, it exists as a matter of degree — you can have a great amount or you can have very little. These degrees of commitment have been classified as: compliance, identification, and internalization.

Compliance, the lowest level of commitment, occurs when an individual hopes to gain certain rewards, but never really shares any special beliefs with the organization. Identification, the next level of commitment, involves maintaining a satisfying organizational affiliation. It is a relationship where an individual may be proud to be a part of the group and respect its values and accomplishments, without necessarily taking the organization's values as his or her own. In contrast, internalization occurs when the values of the organization are congruent with what the individual believes. As a company progresses through the various stages of development, different degrees of commitment are established by people working for the firm. When one starts working for a company, it is normally predicated upon a certain income and working conditions. While not necessarily accepting the organization's values, as a company progresses past the initial

Ownership: What Does It Look Like?

1. Thorough knowledge of the business and continuous efforts to gather new information.
2. Ability to clearly and consistently articulate business goals, objectives, principles, priorities.
3. Involvement in decision making, goal setting, problem solving.
4. Continuous efforts to improve results; never satisfied with OK results.
5. Genuine concern about failures.
6. Major expenditure of time and effort (often at the expense of personal time).
7. Personal follow-up on plans, decisions, actions.
8. Concern about costs, expenses.
9. Concern about the public image of the business.
10. Risk-taking behaviors (to improve business).
11. Relatively high levels of freedom, independence, control.
12. Personal confidence, feelings of importance (which may be viewed by others as arrogance).
13. Self-imposed accountability for results.
14. Ability to link personal efforts (directly or indirectly) to results (success and failures).
15. Concern about members' level of contribution to the business.
16. Willingness to "relax" formal roles or to be flexible when business needs dictate.
17. Initiate in taking actions.

Source: Procter & Gamble

Table 6.1   Ownership: What Does It Look Like?

stages, people respect these values and the relationships that do exist. If a company can develop sufficiently, the level of commitment exists as a mutual sharing of beliefs.

Furthermore, the highest level of development, organizational commitment, involves the psychological process of internalization. With internalization, there are at least three traits characteristic of an individual's commitment to the organization: (1) a strong endorsement of the organization's goals and values, (2) a willingness to exert considerable time and energy on behalf of the organization, and (3) a strong desire to maintain an active membership in the organization. When organizational commitment exists, it influences not only the attitude of a person, but also the person's behavior.

When organizational commitment exists, the dynamics for high productivity are set up because of the mutuality that comes into existence between the individual and the organization. The high productivity arises from the melding of individualistic self- interests and mutually beneficial investments. Because individual self-interest and organizational self-interest are now harmonious, individual actions are willingly and actively taken. The actions taken, which normally incur increasing individual time and energy, are an investment. In addition, as an organization progresses through the stages presented, the company also makes significant investments in the satisfaction of individual needs. This is reflected in the sense of ownership felt by each individual.

In it simplest terms, what we see happening is something that looks like this:

- All people have a self-interest in satisfying their needs (motivation). Furthermore, people are more motivated to preserve and develop that in which they have already made an investment. In other words, the magnitude of self-interest is in direct proportion to the investment already made.

- So, as people come to see an organization as being more their company (increasing ownership) and the more they see success connected to individual efforts (payoff for the individual and investment by the organization), the greater their commitment will be to that company.
- Therefore, the more committed the individuals become to the company (increasing investment), the greater their efforts will be toward its success (future payoffs).

What transpires in this final stage of development, is the establishment of mutuality. A mutuality of self-interest, a mutuality of investment, and a mutuality of success. All receive a return on their investment. In its simple terms, it means that when people are treated like owners, they act like owners.

You Must Look Backward to Go Forward

Fit, direction, and commitment are included together because they are primarily overall organizational issues. While recognition and confidence can be solely an individual initiative, fit, direction, and commitment cannot be. Fit, direction, and commitment have to come from a global perspective to have a lasting effect.

One must not lose sight, however, of the steps necessary to reach the pinnacle of productivity. In fact, the initial three to six months are especially important in determining whether and to what extent the organizational commitment of new members will develop. We have to think about the end of the process at the very beginning. In other words, attention, credibility, integrity, vision, and so forth provide the foundation for commitment. They all must be present. As missing stones in a house's foundation will lead to its eventual collapse, organizational commitment will collapse if its foundation is not solid. And a solid foundation is maintained through consistency and persistence.

CHAPTER SEVEN

So You're Doing It Right, but It's Not Working

———

So You're Doing It Right, but It's Not Working

It is not the going out of port, but the coming in, that determines the success of a voyage.

— Henry Ward Beecher

THIS chapter will explore the issues and problems that confront companies pursuing the development of high-commitment, high-productivity work systems. The opening portion of the chapter will focus on major issues, present questions that have to be answered, and examine dilemmas that have to be resolved before managers can design effective organizational structures and processes. After the issues are discussed, potential problems which impede movement through the various stages of development are considered.

The issues portion of the chapter will be general in nature. It will focus on the basic difficulties that have to be overcome before performance levels that are consistent with high levels of productivity can be achieved. Five themes will be addressed: compensating people, what taking part in the action means, concerns about trust, the impact of organizational maturity, and examining the nature of productivity.

The second part of the chapter will concentrate on barriers

that can hinder a systematic development process for an organization. Each level of development brings increasing productivity along with the promise of even greater returns thereafter. However, each stage also has hidden obstructions. Unless we can identify these potential hazards, the unseen impediments can keep us from progressing to the levels of productivity we desire.

Interests and Anxieties

Issue 1: Money

The issue that will be treated first is one that is invariably brought up first — money. How important is it? How does it fit in? How much should we pay someone?

Money can be viewed in at least three ways. The first and most obvious concern is how much to pay someone for what they are presently doing. The question to consider is whether it should be based on skill or based on contribution. The second monetary consideration is whether people should be given something extra over and above their normal pay? This can be an annual bonus, quarterly bonus, or perhaps some type of gain sharing plan related to productivity. The final area concerning money revolves around whether some kind of safeguard relating to continuity should be provided to individuals. Some companies, such as Lincoln Electric, provide guaranteed employment after a certain trial period. Other companies, while not guaranteeing employment, pretty much guarantee that employment won't be severed solely at the whim of management or with every dip of the economy. At Motorola, as we saw earlier, employees with ten years of service can be terminated only with the approval of Chairman Bob Galvin. In a similar vein, ServiceMaster possesses and enforces quite strict review policies before any individual's employment can be terminated. Furthermore, in addition to its individual review policy, ServiceMaster provides what might be termed an extra measure of security. While many companies give golden parachutes to their top management, ServiceMaster furnishes what it calls silver parachutes to _all_ of its employees. A silver parachute guarantees that everyone will get one year's pay if the company is ever taken over by someone else.

Before we consider any form of compensation, we need to consider the relationship of money to productivity. How important is money as a means of increasing productivity? This topic has been the subject of considerable debate among academics, managers, and consultants.

Some research studies seem to support the position that intangible rewards are what is truly important. Providing actions such as feedback promotes feelings of self-determination and competency within an individual, which in turn results in an increased task motivation. However, it has been pointed out that tangible rewards also can enhance motivation when people see their individual performance as a reflection of their competence. Moreover, the relationship between intangible rewards and tangible rewards has been presented as one that is additive in nature. When a person feels competent in accomplishing his or her work and receives a tangible reward based on performance, the reward appears to heighten that particular individual's level of motivation.

What do all of the research studies mean? When all of the studies are considered together, there seems to be no better resolution after the research is examined than when we started. The fingers point in different directions. Basically, the best that can be said is that there is disagreement about tangible rewards. However, the one point of agreement that is reached — a significant one — is that all of the studies seem to point to the importance of the relationship between self-perceptions of competency and individual motivation. In other words, what occurs throughout the organization's development process (as presented in Chapter 4) and especially in the initial stages, is critical, regardless of any money issues.

Even though the issue of money is unresolved from research findings, in practice, how we pay people appears to be important and needs to be considered because of its symbolic value to people within the organization. Money, in its different forms, represents or signifies fairness, trust, and integrity. Tom Cash, a senior vice-president at American Express, pointedly answers skeptical managers who question why employees should receive anything extra for doing a good job when he states, "We're talking about human beings here, and human beings need to be recognized and rewarded for special efforts." He continues by contending, "You don't even have to give them much. What they want is tangible proof that you really care about the job they do. The reward is really just a symbol of that." When you tell someone that they are valuable, but most of the gains go primarily to top management and the stockholders, then there is a noticeable disparity between what is said and what is actually done. Money is an outcome, a tangible symbol, of the success of the process. Unless the perceptions of money match what is going on in the process, there can be no credibility, trust, or high productivity.

That brings us back to the way that we compensate people. The only right way is what fits the organization. For example, Lincoln Electric uses what is viewed by many as an antiquated piece-rate system of pay. But in addition to the piece-rate pay, there is an annual bonus and guaranteed employment. There is no right system. There is only one that is seen as being honest and fair — as it is at Lincoln.

While no one system is right for all situations, two points appear to be key in the development of a system of compensation. First, it is essential to tie rewards to individual performance. They are not separate matters. The disparity between rewards and performance in the current business environment was cited in the report by Public Agenda Foundation. The commentary provided on this point is that "one of the most startling findings of the national survey of working Americans is the degree to which the American workplace has undercut the link between a jobholder's pay and his or her performance. This situation represents a sharp departure from the traditional American value of individualism. A central theme of our cultural heritage supports the idea that individuals will fail or succeed through their own effort and hard work. When people receive equal rewards regardless of effort or achievement, the implicit message from management is: 'We don't care about extra effort, so why should you?'" The second point is that significant thought needs to be given to tangible rewards, apart from the individual considerations just discussed, and how they fit into the organization process itself. The harmony of the tangible and intangible rewards is an affirmation of the process itself. So, how we pay people is not as simple as it is often treated. The real implications of pay and pay systems within the organization should not be underestimated.

Issue 2: Participation

What we have presented thus far in the book is essentially a model of progressive recognition and attention. The frequency, intensity, and types of recognition and attention change and build upon each other as a company progresses through the different stages of development. Starting out with simple forms of recognition, we move to recognizing each person's unique capabilities and fitting or integrating them into the operations of the organization. The issue of money just discussed is one form of recognition. It can probably be described quite accurately as a symbolic reinforcer of other events and activities taking place in the organization. However, money provides just one means of recognition and, by itself, does not really provide anything more than a relatively low level of commitment. To gain the level of commitment necessary for high productivity, recognition other than that provided by money needs to be addressed. This recognition comes from participation in the process.

While frequently used as a catchall term, participation comes in a variety of forms each of which is important to an organization's operation. "First, employees may participate in *setting goals*. Second, they may participate in *making decisions*, choosing from among alternative courses of action. Third, employees may participate in *solving problems* — a process that includes the definition of issues and the generation of alternative courses of action, as well as choice among the alternatives. Finally, participation may involve *making changes* in the organization." As we view the distinct participation possibilities available for an individual, we see that the different kinds of participation relate not only to recognition, but also to the quality of ownership experienced by an individual within an organization.

Consequently, participation becomes the limiting factor in attaining productivity. Traditional organizations allow little or no participation and exhibit levels of productivity that can be good, fair, or poor depending upon the technological intensity of the organization. Companies allowing some participation can have somewhat higher levels of productivity which may show up in the marketplace, on the bottom line, or not at all. Companies that allow significant participation can create shared visions, excitement, and purpose within individuals. Only organizations that allow each person to have a hand in changing the organization can experience a sense of ownership and build a significant strategic advantage.

There is a downside to participation, however, in that it must be constantly monitored. The emergence of participation symbolizes a mutual respect and trust within the organization. However, mutual respect can quite easily degenerate. What makes monitoring it so tough is that the degeneration is gradual and, therefore, may go unrecognized until it is too late to stop it. When mutual respect loses its genuine mutuality, we literally lose the participation of one or both of the parties. What we finally get in one form or another is one of the following:

- benevolent paternalism
- do anything you want
- indecision

Each of these degenerate forms has its own set of problems; however, all that is important is that productivity decreases and what was worked for diligently in the past is probably lost. A second aspect to be monitored is that of ensuring that each individual gets a return for his or her investment. As organizations utilize greater forms of participation, they tend to rely more on groups or teams to make decisions and, in general, become initiators of action. The groups or teams become the source of the power, but the individual also needs recognition that doesn't destroy the integrity or cohesiveness of the group. Each individual, on an individual basis and apart from the group, has to receive a return for investment of time and energy or else that investment will slowly be withdrawn and put in other places that do provide a return.

Issue 3: Trust

Failure to provide attention usually occurs as the result of oversight rather than being consciously withheld. In contrast, a lack of trust is something about which most people are quite aware.

Why do people fail to develop trust in their relationships? Unfortunately, many people share the following beliefs about what happens as a result of creating trust:

- We will have less control over what is going on.
- We will suffer a loss of respect from peers or subordinates.
- We will have less power.
- We may lose a critical competitive edge.
- It wastes valuable time.
- We may be taken advantage of by other people.
- We will become more open to criticism.
- We will appear indecisive.

What are the consequences of mistrust? The negative impact can be viewed equally well from both organizational perspectives — bottom and top. From the bottom, people do not have trust in their organization because they do not feel they have received their fair share and even feel that they are viewed as expendable commodities. From the top, individuals aren't trusted because it is felt they don't give their best efforts, they don't understand or care what was going on, and, perhaps, they might even steal something.

Trust is an important issue because it is something that *must* prevail before people within an organization will recognize that any mutual objectives actually exist. Managers will allow subordinates to participate in running the business only if they believe that the subordinates will function responsibly. Non-management people will take part only if they have confidence that the organization will not exploit them or that they will not be punished for honest mistakes. Within an organization, individuals will support each other only if they can rely on the fact that others will respond in a similar fashion.

Building trust is a rigorous process that can only develop over time and can be wiped out by merely one action. While trust is established in the early phases of development, it must be continually reinforced and magnified in the later phases. Each individual or organizational action either builds upon or reduces the effect of previous actions. Granting personal autonomy, sharing sensitive operating information, and supporting individual development represent tangible expressions of good faith and intent, in addition to providing particularly potent symbolism of what the organization stands for. The environment of trust leads to free and open communication and enables an environment to exist where a high level of commitment can flourish.

Issue 4: Maturity

Many organizations seem to have a life cycle. During this life cycle, the organization exhibits growth, maturity, decline and, inevitably, demise. Several questions become relevant. Why does it happen? How does it happen? And finally, does it have to happen?

In the typical organization, at one time or another, the

philosophies and goals of the organization are clear. In addition, there is generally an architect who has decisive ideas about what is to be achieved and how to go about doing it. The well-being of the firm can continue for a long period of time as long as it is experiencing growth, and the influence of the original architect remains a part of the organization. During this period, the organization develops the various structures necessary to meet its goals. At some point though, the organization ceases to grow. Over time, identity with the original philosophies and goals wanes. As a consequence, the systems developed and the rules that people follow begin to take on a life of their own, rather than assisting in actual organizational growth. As the people become further enmeshed in following procedures, the raison d'etre for performing any activity becomes "that's the way we do things around here." The business environment, customers and competitors, and perhaps even the original founding philosophies may no longer have any relevance to the way the organization actually operates.

The preceding consequences are invariably also accompanied by a common pattern of structural evolution. This pattern has been referred to as the "functional silo syndrome." (See Table 7.1.) This is, in general, why the life cycle happens.

If what happens is so clear, why doesn't someone stop it? Mainly because they aren't aware that it is happening. This lack of awareness is known by different names, such as the dinosaur syndrome or the boiled frog syndrome. If we put a frog in some water and gradually raise the temperature, the frog will not realize it is slowly being cooked until it is too late. Organizations, like the frog or dinosaurs, do not recognize what is going on until it is too late. Put in terms of the model presented in Chapter 4, attention disappears, credibility and integrity become lost, vision blurs, and direction is lacking or

Functional Silos and Today's Organizations

In their development, many companies create an organizational structure based upon functional specialties (i.e. production, marketing, finance etc.). During this process, these functional areas tend to develop tall hierarchies and become isolated from the other functions within the organization, hence the characterization of a company as a group of silos. An operating definition of organizations with company silos is provided by M. Scott Myers as follows:

Separate identities for separate functional specialties. Loyal to function first; company second.

Closed cultures for each silo. Internally-used "buzzwords" make it difficult for outsiders to comprehend silo activities.

Competitors are viewed as other silos almost as much as other companies. At worst, it results in blame-passing and negative politics by ladder climbers.

Stymied learning results from siloists dissociating themselves from problems to avoid blame. As an organization, the forest of silos has a learning dysfunction.

Protected sovereignty has become a silo's way of life. Internal measurements and rewards perpetuate it. Horizontal integration is seen as a threat—unless another function is absorbed.

When working inside a functional silo, the people would tend to experience the following kinds of perceptions:

We are confused about the organization's key priorities. Conflicting forces tug at us, so we feel no real sense of direction.

Very little straightforward business information is shared. We do not know the real problems. Thus, we just do not know what we should work on.

We are "so distant" from the executives who make the operating decisions about our jobs that we have no feelings of trust or influence.

We seldom interact with anyone from another function. We do not really know what they do. We just stay out of trouble with our own bosses.

All the big bosses care about are the numbers.

Our jobs are so narrow, repetitive, and boring that most days it takes a major mental effort just to go to work.

We never seem to take time to find the real causes of problems. We just error-detect, error-correct.

We rely on legalistic rules rather than a set of broad operating principles everyone should live up to.

We continually hear about problems our customers have. Why can't we meet with them ourselves to learn what we are doing wrong?

Adapted from "Organizational Renewal: Tearing Down the Functional Silos" AME Study Group on Functional Organization, *Target*, Summer 1988, p. 4-14.

Table 7.1   Functional Silos and Today's Organizations

not definitive. Therefore, the sense of ownership dissipates over time, and commitment weakens or is lost.

Does it have to happen? Yes, if we follow the script presented above. Traditionally, we define what we are doing in terms of groups of people rather than as an organization. What this means is that a relatively few people (or perhaps even only one person) become responsible for what goes on. Therefore if the architect or architects of the system leave, die, or simply become interested in something else, the organization that was created generally ends up following the typical life cycle. However, when we view the organization as a whole, everyone becomes responsible and is, therefore, concerned about what is going on. The managers no longer function as monitors or police, because the process and the values become one with the people in the organization. Whether or not an organization follows a traditional life cycle is a function of who owns what is going on. Is it a few people or is it many? Does having many owners guarantee productive companies? Again, no, but it certainly makes it easier for a company to stay on course.

What can be done to make sure that organizations do not fall prey to the life cycle? Actions that have been taken to keep organizations robust and vibrant basically fall into two types. One type is the development of a sensing system. An organizational sensing system provides data on the health and vitality of the organization. The system reports on a regular and sometimes even a continuous basis about what is happening in the system. One such system exists at the Best Foods plant discussed earlier where there is essentially a network of major plant-wide operating committees, one of which is the Social System Support Task Force. It interprets and develops plant norms. Other organizations have developed less formal, but still quite effective, means for examining what is actually happening. The second action relates what is going on to what should be going on. This occurs by periodically examining the vision and linking it to current organizational objectives. In other words, we look at whether we are going in the direction that we want to go. To see if we are heading in the right direction, the following questions need to be answered: Are our day-to-day actions getting us to where we want to go? Are we living the vision? It is much easier to live the rules and procedures. If the rules and procedures become disconnected from the vision, we end up doing things but not accomplishing what we desire.

Issue 5: Productivity

All organizations in America can increase their productivity by at least 20 percent.

Is this, too, a bold or even a foolhardy statement? No, not really. In fact, it is probably a very conservative statement. In truth, most companies can probably increase their relative productivity by 100 percent to 300 percent. Productivity is a complicated topic, and it is also one which many people can't agree on how to define let alone increase it. How, then, should we proceed in making our organizations better?

By simply recognizing that there is a difference between productivity and control. What it comes down to is answering the question: Do we really want to be productive, or do we merely want to be better? Just being better means, in fact, that we just want more control. What we end up doing is controlling _how people do it_ rather than viewing what is actually more appropriate — _what they accomplish._ We try to control the process rather than the output. What we get is not increased productivity, but fluctuating productivity. When things get tough, we squeeze a bit harder and get a bit more. If we pause

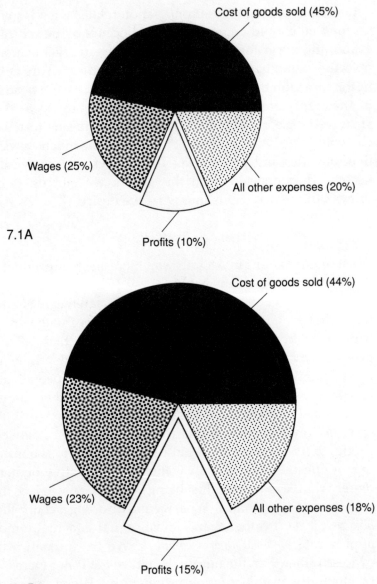

Cost of goods sold (45%)

Wages (25%)

All other expenses (20%)

7.1A

Profits (10%)

Cost of goods sold (44%)

Wages (23%)

All other expenses (18%)

Profits (15%)

7.1B

Figure 7.1   Views of Productivity

for a moment and think about the last statement, we will realize that every time we squeeze we get more productivity. It is always there! What is even more important to realize is that we don't have to go through all the aggravation of squeezing, and we can get even more. All we have to do is to see productivity for what it really is.

Productivity can be thought of in two ways. One way is to do what we are doing by being more demanding. This is what we get by squeezing — working harder. The other way is by doing something that we are not now doing. This is the area we don't squeeze but that has much more to give. This second view of productivity refers to using our discretionary time, being innovative, and creating a new environment. One view of productivity is not better than the other. Both are utilized in the genuinely productive organizations.

It's easier to understand the difference between the two aspects of productivity if we think in terms of a pie chart. The first way of thinking about productivity looks at how the pie is divided up and attempts to make the portion going to profits larger. (See Figure 7.1A.) The second way of thinking about productivity attempts not only to make the portion going to profits larger, but invariably also tends to make the whole pie larger. (See Figure 7.1B.)

In the preceding chapter, I discussed how we really limit productivity gains when we do not consider factors such as discretionary time. We generally don't deal with such considerations because we don't know how to measure them. So what do we do? Ignore them, of course, and focus our attention exclusively on the things that we can measure. The crucial point about high productivity is that just because we don't have good ways of measuring certain effects, it doesn't mean that we should neglect them.

I started this section by stating corporate America can

increase productivity by at least 20 percent. On what basis do I make this statement? I make this claim from one simple statement. During my visit to Lincoln Electric, Richard Sabo, vice-president of public relations, said that Lincoln could probably increase its productivity by about 20 percent. The impact of that statement astounded me. Here I was at one of the most productive, if not the most productive, companies in America and a member of its top management team states that it can be substantially better. This comment about a lean Lincoln makes one pause to consider how much slack really is present in most of our companies today.

Puzzles and Predicaments

Aside from the general issues presented, one has to be cognizant of the specific problems that plague the development of an organization. Even though the basis for achieving high performance is understood, it is important to watch for barriers and obstacles. These barriers and obstacles are readily recognizable because they manifest themselves in much the same way as they would in an individual who is experiencing a physical illness or distress. When a disorder goes unrecognized in an organization, it effectively keeps the organization from proceeding to higher levels of development and productivity. The consequence is plateauing or possibly even backsliding. These disorders are illustrated in Figure 7.2.

During the attention phase, if status differences between people remain, subordinates will not see themselves as real parts of the organization, but as the same old cogs in the wheels of corporate activity. Individuals will come to realize that rather than contributing to the organization they are being used by the organization. The attention that was given initially will gradually be viewed as false or hollow, and it will be perceived that everyone is being manipulated — a means to an end. When problems occur at the beginning, it is similar to a human who doesn't get enough proper nutrients and suffers anemia. Just as anemic people are tired all of the time, lack energy, and do not operate at a very efficient pace, so are the people in these organizations. In the worst case, alienation or a sense of apathy may also develop.

In the confidence phase, if people do not function interde-

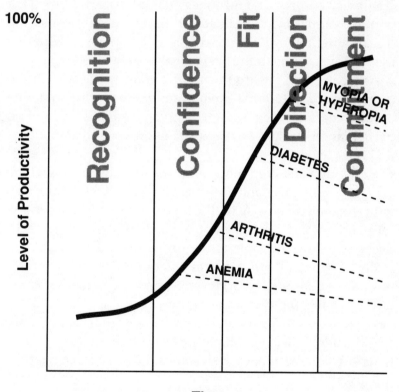

Figure 7.2   Potential Problems

pendently, that is, if they remain relatively insulated or independent of each other, the attention that was showered upon them will be seen as being meaningless because people will not develop the necessary levels of trust. The feeling that will develop, whether accurate or inaccurate, is that something is being hidden. When this occurs, what develops can best be referred to as corporate arthritis. Companies become inflexible and rigid because it is easier and safer to do what we have been doing all along. From an overall perspective, credibility is not just being honest, it is actively providing the current realities to subordinates. If the situation becomes too threatening, the cynicism that may develop could wipe out the positive effects of the first stage.

As we proceed toward the middle of the process, we try to create an organizational orientation for the individual. The problem occurs when a vision is given from the top, and no participation is sought or required of others in the organization. We develop what might be termed corporate diabetes. The attention and credibility stages create a headiness where everyone feels good, and now there is a grandiose dream to go with the good feeling. Actually, there is a great self-deception for people at the top, at the bottom, and in between. The self-deception for the people at the top is that the vision is not really a vision but only a dream that may be partially carried out, carried out poorly, or never carried out at all. For others farther down the corporate ladder, it is a euphoria. They never leave their dream world for the world of reality, until reality rudely awakens them. Just as a human body suffers when an overabundance of sweetness is ingested, so does the organization.

As we move from producing the "corporate fit" to providing direction, the major requirement becomes one of maintaining balance. If we emphasize the focusing aspect of direction too much, we become a myopic or shortsighted organization. This is fine if we have no competitors. But myopia inevitably creates competitors, if they are not already there. Conversely, if we don't provide enough focus and overemphasize the developmental part of direction, we end up with hyperopia or farsightedness. When the emphasis is solely on the future, things of here and now tend to get done inefficiently. Again, we create our own competitors from those companies that provide more and better value for our customer's current needs.

The pursuit of high performance and productivity is fraught with many obstacles, even in the best of organizations. Ideally, each organization should be its own doctor, diagnose its own symptoms, and write its own prescription. Going to outside specialists (consultants) is an alternative, but it should be remembered that the outside specialist might have a different frame of reference and might needlessly extend the period of recuperation.

Solution Through Resolution

The preceding play on words emphasizes the need for companies to recognize the game in which they play. The rules of the game are different for each company. Just as companies differ in competitors and customers, so too, in the games in which they play. It is equally important to recognize that, even if we have the same competitors and customers, the game we are in is probably not quite the same as the ones our competitors are playing.

The focus of this chapter is on identifying underlying issues and problems. Unless the issues and problems are well thought through and some form of resolution reached, complications will surely result. The complications can materialize as overt conflict or can remain under the surface as unresolved conflict. In either case, the conflict will not be productive conflict and the organization will be adversely affected. The issues, problems, and paradoxical situations that may arise have to be recognized and resolved appropriately or else the implementation of a wide range of productivity programs will be impossible.

CHAPTER EIGHT

Tales to be Told

Tales To Be Told

*If one advances confidently in the direction of his dreams, and
endeavors to lead the life which he has imagined, he will meet
with a success unexpected in common hours.*

— Henry David Thoreau

I N Chapter 7, a discussion en-
sued on the issue of produc-
tivity. The basic idea that should come from the discussion is
that we can become more productive not by adding more but
by getting more of what is already there. The increased productivity comes not just from squeezing tighter but from
reaching higher. Further elaboration needs to be made to
understand how this makes a company productive. Most of
the time, when we speak of productivity, we speak of it
unilaterally in terms of the organization. To be successful,
however, there needs to be a mutuality of perspective.

Mutuality in a company implies that there is a process of
exchange taking place. "The employee gives his or her abilities and efforts to the organization, and in exchange, the
organization rewards the employee for such efforts. Managers spend much of their energies trying to maximize the
employee's contributions to the organization without duti-
fully attending to the other side of the exchange process —

ensuring that those rewards are valued at a maximum by employees." The unilateral view, thinking only in terms of the company so prevalent in today's organizations, creates an environment that is conducive only to short-term "bursts" of productivity. When the contributions are perceived as being too much in favor of the company, productivity stops or even reverses until the next set of incentives — or disincentives, as the case may be — comes along. How a company resolves basic issues such as money, participation, and trust will define the degree of contribution by the organization, or from the perspective of the organizational members, the rewards they receive. How people perceive the rewards that they are given (non-financial as well as financial) will, in large measure, determine the level of motivation and satisfaction within individuals.

This chapter will highlight distinctive programs or distinctive system-wide changes that companies are employing to reach higher and increase the productivity of their organizations. The emphasis in these distinctive actions is that it is being done in a way that is mutually satisfying to all parties involved. What differentiates most of this chapter from Chapter 2, where we discussed high-performing organizations, is that all of the transformed operations in this chapter are only average or even below-average performers. The emphasis in this chapter is not that change can occur, but that it is literally waiting to happen.

The Importance of Being Earnest

Although this chapter will concentrate primarily on the larger viewpoint, it will start out with an individual and his job. This is being done for two reasons: (1) to clarify what is happening at the micro level, because programs are essentially individual efforts multiplied, and (2) to show that One

Manager's Story was not a quirk but a common event that in most instances only needs recognition.

Ben worked in the warehouse of a Fortune 500 company for more than 20 years. The company was a pretty good company for which to work, as well as one that had been relatively successful. One day, while working at home, Ben suffered an unfortunate accident. This accident created a long-term disability that allowed him to stand for only short periods of time and would not allow him to lift any heavy objects. Ben could no longer do his job in the warehouse. Many companies would have let Ben go. It would have made good economic sense. After all, one Ben was as good as another Ben. This was not the case with Ben's company, which elected to retain him even though his productive capacity was rather severely diminished.

But what could Ben do? A manager was assigned the task of finding Ben something to do. He looked and looked. What he discovered was that the reception desk at the plant entrance was being shared by a group of people. These people took their work with them from their regular work area and did it while they were sitting at the reception desk waiting to receive the infrequent visitors that came to the plant. It was an inconvenience that was shared part-time by several clerical employees. The manager had found the job for Ben! Ben was put at the reception desk and given some additional tasks to do such as checking invoices while he sat and waited for visitors.

Let us stop and analyze this situation. The company certainly did the admirable thing by keeping Ben on as an employee and paying him his wages. In reality, though, the company's return was negative. Ben wasn't earning his pay. Ben was also bored because he had a make-work job in which the thing that he did the most was kill time. What the company did was praiseworthy, but it was not productive for either the company or Ben. Why did this happen? Lack of imagination. According to a definition presented earlier, the manager responsible for finding Ben a job (and other managers in the company, too) failed to see what was actually there. He came up with an answer but not a solution.

Ben's story, however, does not end here. Every day, managers walked by Ben not giving him any more than the usual amount of thought or attention. One day, though, a manager did stop and ask Ben if he could help her. The managers in this plant were conducting workshops relating to the various aspects of running their business. They conducted the workshops while also doing their respective jobs as well as they could. The workshops were very time-consuming because the individuals facilitating the workshops were also responsible for all necessary preparations such as arranging for food, making coffee, and cleaning up afterward. The preparations took as much time and work as the workshops themselves. When they were in charge, the workshop managers had to come in earlier and stay later, while fighting to stay above water on their own jobs.

Back to the manager who asked Ben if he could give her a hand. The reason that she asked Ben was that at the time, she happened to have an even larger regular workload than normal. With that and because she also had to conduct the workshop, the workload was becoming unmanageable, even though she was coming in earlier and staying later. What was Ben's reaction? After all, he didn't work for her. He was excited, he was enthusiastic, but most of all he was grateful to be a part of the action again.

After he completed this particular workshop, Ben volunteered his services to other managers facilitating other workshops. Ben didn't have to do it, but he wanted to do it. Ben continued helping and transformed these mundane activities into "his business" and even developed a system for doing workshops. Ben took a job on which most managers in the plant looked negatively and made it into something that he enjoyed. Not only did he enjoy doing it but he did it better than the managers would have done it themselves.

One instance typifies the intensity of ownership that Ben experienced. During one workshop, the participants didn't like the food and complained. On his own time at home, he called the owner of the restaurant servicing the workshops and worked out a way to modify the food to meet the needs of the people at the workshop.

On days that workshops take place, Ben gets in about an hour earlier than normal, directs the facilitators about what has to be done, and checks on the progress of the workshop several times during the course of the day. On his own, he started putting together the workbooks used in the workshops and started his own individual training program.

Why did Ben do everything that he did? He was getting paid regardless. This was extra effort that he didn't have to put forth — but did anyway. Ben could probably be described as an average worker at this company. He was neither better nor worse than anyone else. He took on the extra activities simply because someone paid attention to what he was doing rather than ignoring him. With this attention, Ben was also given permission to be productive. Ben continued to expand his role because it increased his feelings of self-worth. Ben, in fact, was creating his own vision for the company and was even taking care of his own training at the same time.

Many times subordinates don't do the extra things because, in many ways, their superiors *won't let them*. Instead of being unleashed, productivity is impeded. People are controlled rather than led. Instead of giving people permission, we don't simply ignore them, but we often deny their desire for increased productivity. Why? Because when people become productive, we have to pay attention to them and what they are doing. In most instances, this conflicts with telling people what to do, which is what most managers think their job is. It is certainly much easier to measure people by the yardstick of our own making rather than to assess each person's contributions.

In Retrospect

When the manager who first went to Ben for assistance was asked why she approached someone who did not report to her, she responded that his lack of productivity bothered her. So after talking to his boss, she asked Ben if he would be willing to do more work. The choice was his. She added, "We need to behave as if it is our [the manager's] own company. When we lose sight of that fact, of course, the workers will too." That last comment brings us to the crux of the problem in most companies. While it seems that most people who talk about the lack of productivity lay the blame on the shoulders of blue-collar workers or the clerical people, in almost any large company, it is caused as much, if not more, by the managers. Most managers don't take ownership in their companies, which is why statistics show some new MBAs have three jobs in the first five years after getting their degree. One experience typifies the real problem. When Motorola first tried to implement productivity programs, it experienced problems in implementation. Guess where the problems were. The workers and first-line managers accepted the new standards with relative ease. It was the middle managers who felt that they had to hold on to the old standards if they were going to continue to be rewarded. We have to be careful to create ownership at all levels within the organization.

Uncovering Productivity

The Clark Equipment Company is an international, integrated manufacturer with plants and subsidiaries in four U.S. states and nine different countries. We are interested, however, only in its plant in Georgetown, Kentucky. In 1985, this particular plant implemented a productivity program most typically referred to as a gainsharing program. The impetus for the pursuit and implementation of this program arose out of the challenges confronting Clark Equipment in its business environment from both its domestic competitors and its foreign rivals — most notably from Japan.

As a focal point, Clark presented the notion that its gainsharing program really has more to do with thinking about people and their particular business than as a one-shot effort. For its productivity program to be successful, Clark underscored the necessity of several prominent points to form the basis of its program. These were:

1. To enhance everyone's understanding of key business objectives.
2. To provide incentives for working together as a team to achieve desired results.
3. To provide timely feedback about organizational performance.
4. To provide a way for everyone to share in the company's success.

The program utilized at Clark Equipment was governed by three key interrelated concepts: objectives, communication, and rewards. Objectives, the first concept, recognized the necessity for defining appropriate performance objectives for the business and relevant measurements for assessing whether the objectives were attained. Communication, the second concept, emphasized the requirement for proper and timely communication of information on how well people were performing against the appropriate business objectives. Rewards, the third concept, completed the process by providing an opportunity for the people involved in the operations to share financially in the success of the organization as the objectives were realized.

In Clark's initial consideration of business objectives, several specific measures were identified as appropriate indicators of business performance. These indicators were: operating costs, quality of the product manufactured, timely delivery of the product to customers, and inventory costs. In turn, each of the specific business-performance indicators was further and more explicitly delineated, as is illustrated in Table 8.1.

Communication, the second key concept, provided the crucial coupling between organizational objectives and individual performance. Communication throughout the process

Performance Indicators Used at Clark Equipment Company	
Performance Indicator	**Measure**
cost reduction and control	cost per unit
product quality	demerits based on audits
customer delivery	number of units past due promised date
inventory	monthly measure

Source: *Clark Material Systems Technology Company, 1985 Gainsharing Plan*

Table 8.1   *Performance Indicators Used at Clark Equipment Company*

Gainsharing Payout Schedule			
Gainsharing Performance	**Total Quarterly Payout**		**Approx. Per Capita Payout**
Below 90.0%	$ 0	0%	$ 0
91.0%	$ 71,875	50%	$ 74
92.0%	$ 71,875	50%	$ 74
93.0%	$ 71,875	50%	$ 74
94.0%	$ 71,875	50%	$ 74
95.0%	$107,813	75%	$111
96.0%	$107,813	75%	$111
97.0%	$107,813	75%	$111
98.0%	$107,813	75%	$111
99.0%	$107,813	75%	$111
100.0%	$143,750	100%	$148

Source: Clark Material Systems Technology Company, 1985 Gainsharing Plan.

Table 8.2   Gainsharing Payout Schedule

took place in several different ways. While management developed the program, a cross-section of the employees reviewed the program and provided assistance in developing a communication strategy. After the program was put into action, all employees were kept informed on a timely basis through monthly performance reports on relevant operating data. Lastly, an employee review committee monitored the program and responded to the concerns that arose from the people involved in the program.

Rewards, the last concept, came in the form of a financial distribution to individuals based upon the performance of the entire plant. This final activity tied the whole productivity process together. A process which began from the company's perspective eventually came full circle and concluded with a perspective of mutuality.

Using the communication process again, a schedule was provided on how people would be paid. Expected payouts based on performance were spelled out. Table 8.2 illustrates the per capita payout. Equally important, the document also clearly defined when payouts wouldn't be made, who was eligible, how someone became eligible, and so forth.

Clark exhibits one way the productivity problem can be attacked. As we continue through this chapter, we will see different and, in some aspects more encompassing, ways of making things get better while tackling the bigger problem of making sure they stay better.

Transformations

Today's disposable baby diapers have had, in retrospect, a considerable impact on our lives. Illustrating this point, the disposable diaper was featured as part of a Smithsonian Institution exhibit on products and services that have "revolutionized our lives." The brand-name most widely associated with the disposable diaper and also the product most responsible for its widespread adoption by consumers is Pampers, produced by Procter & Gamble.

The flagship plant of Procter & Gamble for the original Pampers disposable diaper was located in Cheboygan, Michigan. This plant produced millions of Pampers diapers. At its peak, people worked around the clock and still could not keep up with the ever-increasing demand for their product.

Instead of the opportunity it seemed to be, the overwhelming success of Pampers proved to be an unrecognized threat for the Cheboygan plant. As demand increased, competitors sprung up externally and also from within the organization.

Internally, new and more efficient plants were built to capital-
ize on the vast untapped market for disposable diapers.
During the 1970s, everyone seemed to be working hard at the
Cheboygan plant to meet the competition. Yet the results
generally seemed to fall short of the performance of the newer
facilities. During this period, stress seemed to escalate which,
in turn, produced deteriorating interpersonal relationships
and ultimately culminated in an eleven-week work stoppage
in 1975.

After this crippling strike, a comprehensive organizational
assessment was undertaken to appraise the prevailing conditions and their causes. During the seven succeeding years,
changes were made to remedy how people worked and
interacted. While Cheboygan had profound competitive
problems, there was significant movement toward the understanding of requisite improvements. As capacity raced past
demand for disposable diapers, though, Cheboygan was
quickly being shoved into what could only be described as the
marginal category. Consequently, while Cheboygan was
making sizable strides toward greater productivity, the point
was eventually reached where production lines had to be
shut down and once indispensable people became excess
baggage.

The lack of productivity at Cheboygan, it should again be
pointed out, was not due to apathy or lack of concern. In fact,
the people at the Cheboygan plant were committed to the
success of their operation. Thus, the point that became ex-
ceedingly clear during this time was that simply working
harder was no solution to Cheboygan problems.

In 1983, after much deliberation and debate, the fateful
decision was made to move to a technician work system. The
transition to the technician system, however, was not without
anguish. The work structure, as well as the entire way of

thinking and believing, had to be changed. The focus during this transition period was on results. Not that results weren't a concern all along — but now they were everyone's concern. With the rising level of individual involvement, Cheboygan plant manager Dick Burns explains, "The organization itself became more responsive and effective."

Because of a good idea, Cheboygan had prospered initially almost irrespective of whatever went on at the plant. A good idea can almost always carry an organization for a while. But more is always necessary if a company is to maintain or increase levels of prosperity.

At Cheboygan, two key processes were institutionalized so that people understood what had to be done and how to do it. First, there was more sharing of information about what was going on in the business. Everyone got the good news — and everyone got the bad news, too! Information came through in-house publications (memos, newsletters, and so on) and daily business meetings. Second, a "checkbook owner" concept was put into effect, which held people responsible for managing the costs of running the business. It was no longer "us" and "them" — it was just "us".

What changed at Cheboygan? Some examples of what happened can best be seen by looking at a few of the people from the plant:

- *Karen* was a clerk at the Cheboygan plant. With the new work system, however, she took on the responsibility for not only planning production, but also the industrial engineering activities for her work area. Before Karen started doing these activities, they were "manager's" work.

- *Tim* was a technician within the Cheboygan plant. When

a request for new machinery to produce a new product was turned down as being too expensive, Tim and several other technicians set out to create what they wanted. Using a "junkyard" approach, this team took an old converter frame and sought out compatible spare parts for it. Tim and his "project team" designed and built the required production system to produce the Attends underpad at a fraction (about 25 percent) of the original estimated expense.

- *John* was also a technician at the Cheboygan plant. Even though he was not creating new business, he was certainly cut out of the same fabric as the preceding coworkers. John was a technician who disliked much of the dullness and tedium of his job. What did he do? What any other owner would do — he changed it. He and several other technicians redesigned an old case-packing machine. First, John and his associates created a prototype out of extra wood, hardware, tape, and a multitude of helpful suggestions. They then worked with a machinery manufacturing company to construct a new semi-automatic case-packing machine based on their prototype. Eventually it cost $500,000, but that was paid off in just one year. Not only did John make his job better but he had fun doing it. How many people within organizations today can make this claim?

Even though the focus at Cheboygan was directed at results, the critical element was that it was built on a deep respect for people. "For years tremendous amounts of time and energy went into developing rules and procedures for making decisions. This rule-oriented decision making created barriers to using innovation and creativity in solving problems in a rapidly changing business environment." The Cheboygan plant traveled a long way in a span of only five years. It experienced not just survival but rejuvenation in almost every sense. How good were the results within the five-year period? Profit margins and cash flows improved during each of the five years with the 1987–1988 period showing the plant's best financial results ever. The plant had increased its productivity and competitiveness by more than one-third. More importantly, everyone realized that there was no resting on one's laurels: Performance had to improve — continually.

More and More

The results at Procter & Gamble's Cheboygan plant are a phenomenon that can occur anywhere, the only *caveat* being that a company must want it to occur. The All Committed to Excellence (ACE) program at Digital Electronics Corporation's Albuquerque plant testifies to the fact that productivity and profits are there just waiting to be taken.

The ACE program, which is based on education, feedback, and rewards, has a no less impressive track record than the preceding example. The process in Albuquerque revolves around Volunteers In Action (VIA) teams. They focus on issues about quality but always end up with many more such as customer satisfaction, improvement ideas, and so forth. The goals of the process are quite simple. As VIA Coordinator Ron Brooks puts it, "People need to know what to do and be given the techniques to do so." But this is just the first step, not the end as some companies assume. Ron Brooks points out that two more steps are needed to complete the process. He says the second step is that "people should be allowed to use what they have been given," a crucial step often never accomplished. The final step in the process is that "people should want to use what they have been given." Employee groups as well as individuals in the plant are recognized and rewarded for their accomplishments. Although there are formal team awards, whenever a "celebration" seems appropriate, a team can be recognized by a 90-minute luncheon. Individuals receive certificates, cash, days off, and recognition for their efforts in a site newspaper and on Digital's "Wall of Fame." What has ACE done for the Albuquerque plant? The results of a pilot study over a two-year period show the following:

- Throughput time was reduced from 6 weeks to 3 days.
- The percentage of defects fell from 15 to 3 percent.
- Direct labor per unit declined by nearly 40 percent.
- Customer service changed from shipping-from-stock in 13-15 weeks to shipping-to-order in just 30 days.

At the time of this review, less than half of the employees (workers, managers, everybody) had been trained in the VIA concept. Viewing the results of the current pilot project, we can easily see the reality, not just the potential, of the ACE program.

Not Just Manufacturing but also Service!

In the fast-food business, conventional wisdom says success comes from increasing the number of business units, that is restaurants. With the increase in units come growing sales and profits. While adding units certainly has the potential for improved sales and profits, in most instances, it merely creates a life cycle. Becoming better off through newer units tends to get offset by older, degenerating units experiencing the declining phase of their life cycle. As the increase in units slows down so does profitability. To stave off the inevitable, more rigorous and advanced cost-control measures are employed. The result only postpones the inevitable.

Yet while many fast-food organizations inevitably have these typical results, there is McDonald's. How does McDonald's prosper? What is the secret that few other chains seem to recognize? The secret is that McDonald's understands that increasing units is only one part of the profit story. Rather than looking at a successful McDonald's, however, we will examine another fast-food chain. This company followed the conventional wisdom but had the insight to recognize that what it was doing wasn't working or, at best, was only providing illusory gains. Ironically, even the new units were not performing at expected levels of performance.

What this company did was undertake an experiment. In much the same manner that companies test market products or services, this company test marketed an idea. We will examine that idea and its results.

The first problem confronting management was which unit to use in its experiment. At first, one might want to look at poor performers. However, just by cleaning up bad conditions one might conceivably achieve gains — even sizable gains and still be unable to retain them. Likewise, top performers were not chosen because there was a concern whether the process, if successful in top performers, could be transplanted effectively to other units. What are we left with? Right — average performers. Therefore, an average performing unit was selected for the experiment and was compared to over 30 other comparable company units in the same area.

The experimental unit was subjected to a broad range of changes that were basically atypical in the fast-food business. The basic system modifications applied to the experimental unit are shown in Table 8.3.

While the changes taking place were great, so were the results. Over a three-year period, the experimental unit

Changes in the Experimental Unit System

Modifications	From → → → →	To
work design	individual	team
decision making	top down rules	mutually developed rules
	management initiated	individual or team involvement
communication	top down	all directions
	selective	everything critical to performance and success
education	secondary and limited in scope	joint responsibility that is encouraged and rewarded
pay	hourly	salaried
	predominantly seniority	degree of development
	poor link to performance	economic gain-sharing

Adapted from "An Example of Economic Gainsharing in the Restaurant Industry," by Donald O. Jewell, and Sandra F. Jewell, National Productivity Review, *V6N2, Spring 1987, pp. 136-137. Reprinted with permission. Copyright © 1987 by Executive Enterprises, Inc., 22 West 21st Street, New York, NY 10010-6904. All Rights Reserved.*

Table 8.3   *Changes in the Experimental Unit*

increased both the number of customers per week (about 19 percent) and the average dollar sale per customer (about 25 percent) which boosted overall profits by nearly 25 percent over the average performance of control units (comparable units with no change taking place). In addition, as a by-product of the experiment, employee turnover was almost 15 percent less than at the control units.

Some Practical Questions

While the gospel according to each of the companies in this chapter is exhilarating, the problems encountered in each particular situation were sometimes seen as never-ending. Even under the best of circumstances, creating change is never easy. When change is instituted within an existing work system, additional and different problems inevitably seem to become part of the package. Although the preceding chapter discussed common issues and problems in trying to develop high performance, there are still additional practical comments and questions that tend to surface in existing organizations exhibiting a diversity of views.

Practical Question #1

Everybody seems to agree with what is said. Yet, when it actually comes to the day-to-day activities, people either don't do the things they are supposed to or else they do them poorly. Why?

When new systems are implemented, there is always resistance. Sometimes it is overt. Sometimes it is covert. Sometimes it is conscious. Sometimes it is unconscious. There are numerous reasons and behaviors all emerging from the same source — uncertainty. And because individuals interpret the uncertainty differently, diverse and dysfunctional reactions occur.

Sally Pearson, a Procter & Gamble manager, has made some observations about what can happen. When a new system comes on-line, she says, "Sometimes something similar to the mourning or grieving process that occurs when a person dies can be experienced." This grieving process can create a tension-filled, often negative atmosphere. To counteract the negative qualities, people's focus must be changed. This refocusing can come directly from the people and their interactions, advance as a result of the external environment, or be inhibited as a result of organizational actions. First, she emphasizes the necessity for recognizing "fixing-the-blame versus working-the-issues" interactions among people. One recurring theme she recounts is that "when people go through change, there is a tendency for individuals to try to fix blame on each other for what went wrong." She warns that a manager must always ensure that blame-fixing behavior is stopped and stopped quickly. This allows people to return to working the real issues; that is, looking forward and not backward.

Recognizing that an external stimulus sometimes can energize a group, she says, "Organizations that have direct competitors (either internal or external) seem to get on line faster." Why do external factors make a difference? Probably because goals become clearer or more focused, thus creating a yardstick for performance. Lastly, she notes that a certain stability has to be maintained during the change process so that desired actions and attitudes are adopted. She cautions, "If you develop a good system, don't allow it to become just a training ground for managers going other places."

Practical Question #2

What if I try to do the right things but the people higher up in the organization want to keep the status quo?

The short, simple answer is that you have to grab their attention. If the higher-ups don't eventually buy into the process, whatever the individual manage does will become a frustrating and thankless process. So how do you grab the attention of those higher in the organization? One of the best and most practical ways is presented in the onion patch strategy. (See Table 8.4.) Basically, it is a recommendation to try not to do too much, too fast, but be ready when the occasion arrives — and then move quickly. Don't make it "my" good idea but "our" good idea. The more people we can "hook into" our idea, directly or indirectly, the greater the base to accomplish more later.

Practical Question #3

When the system changes, I'll probably have to take on the jobs of one or two other people. How is this possible?

This is a common fear but it doesn't necessarily have to become a traumatic work episode. Two remarks are particularly relevant to the above question. First, since so much effort is put into designing new systems, sometimes much less effort is put into implementing them. But design and implementation are really two connected issues. Any system can look good on paper. Only when you take it out for a "test drive" can you tell what will happen. Substantial effort is needed after the initial design to allow people to understand what will actually happen as opposed to what they think will happen.

Secondly, many times so much attention is focused on the blue-collar or clerical workers that much less energy is spent on defining the manager's "new role" *and* helping the manager change. This is especially true for older managers who have lived and acted under different sets of rules. What ends

The Onion Patch Strategy

What can be done when your company's top managers are not quality leaders and champions? When you are a lone quality champion without support of top leadership — a "lonely little petunia in an onion patch"? In general, the onion patch strategy is: "Think big, but stay close to your roots." Select improvement efforts within your span of control — but select improvements that capture the attention of people at least two links up in the chain of command. Look for projects with "big dollar" implications. For example, projects that reduce waste or rework, or increase sales or revenue. Concentrate your efforts on achieving the kind of results that others, even skeptics, will respect. Include other people in your efforts. Include even more people in the sharing of credit for a successful job. Build a network of believers and supporters while you make real improvements in the system.

Sometimes you will have direct supervisory responsibility over people involved in improvement efforts. If so, shield them from outside pressures so that they can continue the work of improving quality.

Be patient and persistent. If you succeed you may create opportunities to introduce the wider implications of quality to higher and higher levels of the organization. Meanwhile, prepare for any opportunities. Be ready to pounce when a mover and shaker asks for information or suggestions. Have at hand copies of books, articles, or videotapes of various lengths that are suitable introductory materials for your managers.

Have prepared an introductory presentation that is flexible enough to fit time slots ranging from 15 to 90 minutes. Have your presentation rehearsed and ready to go. Include, among your presenters, hourly operators who have become zealots for the new way. They need not be slick or articulate. Their excitement will be eloquence enough.

Identify the most common questions or objections and be prepared to respond to them. Figure out ways to persuade your managers to hear the quality leaders speak. Compile success stories. Prepare them in a "picture book" format that is easy to follow and loaded with graphics. Ask the resisters to help out on some quality activity.

The onion patch transformer must keep in mind that his or her efforts should always be geared to getting the attention of top management, educating them, and making believers and champions of them. Without their eventual buy-in, all of your transformation efforts will wither on the vine.

Adapted from "Beginning the Quality Transformation, Part 1," by Peter R. Scholtes and Heero Hacquebord, Quality Progress, *July 1988, p. 32. Joiner Associates, Inc. © 1987.*

Table 8.4   The Onion Patch Strategy

up happening is embodied in the comment of a manager living in a post-change environment. "Since my time is limited now," he said, "I make choices about what is important and can no longer afford to look at the numbers 18 different ways." Change is a disruption in everyone's life. It makes people uncomfortable and threatens their security. But as the preceding quote states, it also gives people more choices and more control over their work environment. Change is both a threat and an opportunity. Successful organizations and managers make sure everyone is aware of both aspects.

To Be or Not to Be...

When questioned about a new product introduction as it related to competition with Japan, an IBM executive responded by saying that the company was not competing against Japan, but competing against other companies. This comment brings into perspective why we are suffering from many of the problems that we are. The following of Japanese businesses and their practices has reached almost mythic proportions as companies grasp for techniques or quick fixes that will miraculously cause a turnaround. The reason why more than a few companies that have quality circles and other techniques have failed is because they have taken a small part of a process.

The companies in this chapter saved millions of dollars by a series of small activities that basically just included people — the resource traditionally left out. These companies took "One Manager's Story" from Chapter 5 and multiplied it several times. Any money saved is really unrecognized profit. The money was always there, but now it can be used for new product development, introducing a new product, or buying a new machine. All of these possibilities are essentially free or, more precisely, ignored. Lincoln Electric's success, in fact,

DO's and DON'T's for Stimulating Worker Commitment and Quality Performance

DO tie remuneration directly to performance that enhances the efficiency and effectiveness of the enterprise.

DO give public and tangible recognition to people who keep standards of quality and effort that exceed average satisfactory job performance.

DO accept wholeheartedly the principle that employees should share directly and significantly in overall productivity gain (however defined).

DO encourage job holders to participate with management in defining recognizable goals and standards against which individual performance can be judged.

DO give special attention to the difficulties that middle managers face in supporting and enforcing programs to restructure the work place.

DO NOT permit situations to develop where the interests of employees run counter to the well-being of the firm — e.g., between introducing technology in a way that threatens employees' job security or overtime.

DO NOT attempt to improve standards of quality unless you are prepared to accept its full costs — e.g., discarding substandard products, paying more for better components, or transferring or dismissing people who cannot do quality work.

DO NOT permit a significant gap to develop between management rhetoric and the actual reward system — nothing feeds employee cynicism as much as management blindness or insincerity about the forms of behavior that really "pay off."

DO NOT pretend that programs designed to increase productivity are really intended to enhance job satisfaction and the dignity of work.

DO NOT support special privileges for managers that serve to enhance the status of managers by widening the gap between them and those who do the work — e.g., giving bonuses to managers at the same time that employees are being laid off.

Source: Yankelovich, Daniel and Immerwahr, John. Putting the Work Ethic to Work, New York: The Public Agenda Foundation, 1983, p. 7.

Table 8.5   DOs and DON'Ts for Stimulating Worker Commitment and Quality Performance

comes from not ignoring what shouldn't be ignored. It gets maximum productivity from its people. And Lincoln not only has money to give back as bonuses to the people who create the productivity, there is enough left over to provide what is necessary in other areas of the organization.

The secret of Japanese companies is not that they are Japanese. Their secret is that they understand what productivity is. The Just-In-Time (JIT) inventory practice we are taking from the Japanese has been used successfully by Lincoln for decades without any fanfare or acclaim. It just happens to be part of Lincoln's system. A summary of the "Do's" and "Don't's" for high productivity are presented in Table 8.5.

Are the companies in this chapter and other parts of the book unique? Only if you want them to be.

CHAPTER NINE

Milestones and Millstones

———

Milestones and Millstones

A wise Man begins in the end; a Fool ends in the beginning.
— Thomas Fuller

S KEPTICAL executives are asking whether there is any substance beneath all the hoopla being generated today as they observe one company after another faltering that once was declared excellent. Were these companies ever really excellent in the first place? Or have they lost some undefinable quality? Or are they suddenly doing things the wrong way? While it could be all of these things, I don't think it is any of them. What it comes down to is simply understanding strategic management.

As competition, the legal system, and creating new customers have become tougher, greater attention is being concentrated on the strategic aspects of a company. Books and articles present an assortment of theoretical and pragmatic explanations of how companies can think and act strategically and prosper. With the variety of explanations present, how do we discern what needs to be done?

In many quarters, strategic management has come to mean increasing shareholder value, viewing businesses as cash cows or stars, and in some instances it has even come to mean figuring out how to take over another company. All of these actions certainly provide a means of growth, but what kind of growth is it? In each of the preceding depictions of strategic management, the focus was on acquiring markets or physical assets. But when viewed in this restricted way, markets and physical assets are only possessions and nothing more. These types of possessions can be undervalued and acquiring them only means good investment, not good management. What many of the views of strategic management fail to provide is an understanding of value and how to create it — the only real reason for any organization to exist. Genuine strategic management is taking this value-creating ability and making it an advantage for your company. When such advantages are created, a company becomes different and better — better than its competitors and better for its customers. Only when a company understands the difference between better and bigger, however, can prosperity exist in the longer term.

Advantages: Apparent and Otherwise

This book has focussed on productivity through building the organization. This view of productivity is one means of formulating value regardless of who the customers might be or what products or services they might require. It is not that we shouldn't care who the customers are or what they want to purchase. Rather, it means being able to serve our customers, whoever they may be, more effectively than our competitors can serve them. In Chapter 1, people utilization was called a strategic advantage. While the strategic advantage is quite important, there is another type of advantage that influences a company's well-being. It is the competitive advantage. Only when one differentiates between these two types of advantages can there be an understanding of why excellent companies may not always be successful companies. And, only when one differentiates between the two types of advantages can there be an understanding of how to turn immediate success into sustained success.

Strategic Advantages

A strategic advantage creates an entitlement for an organization that cannot be duplicated easily — or even duplicated at all. The way we develop our organization and use people productively is one type of strategic advantage. Developing a certain level of technical knowledge or expertise is another type of strategic advantage. Creating a proprietary process also can be a strategic advantage.

Developing an organization that fully utilizes the people within it is a rather unique strategic advantage in that one company can never do exactly the same as another. Each company can make its own version, which might be better or worse than another company's version but never the same. While it is a sweeping generalization, it is probably quite accurate to say that developing the organization is in some way connected to most other strategic advantages. For example, if a company distinguishes itself from its competitors by a particular technical expertise, it probably occurred as much because it provided an environment where this expertise was allowed to exist as from any particular skill or insight exhibited by any person or group of people within the company.

While strategic advantages can provide a competitive edge, having them in no way guarantees that a company actually will have a competitive edge. It provides a means to be successful but not a guarantee. If we have a patent but another company develops a new technology, then the patent doesn't mean very much. Likewise, in an organization with a highly-committed work force that operates very productively, if we do not provide what the customers need, the strategic advantage becomes largely an apparent advantage. To be successful, strategic advantage has to become functional. To become functional, we must transform strategic advantage into competitive advantage.

Competitive Advantages

At the business unit level, we speak in terms of markets and competitors. Most businesses try to develop some kind of competitive edge. This competitive edge comes from recognizing the connections among producing a product or service, delivering that product or service, and satisfying a customer's needs. A competitive advantage is understanding and using a particular business relationship better than your competitors can. A competitive advantage can come within any of the functional areas of a business. It might mean understanding that a plant of larger scale will allow prices to be lower than those of the competition. It might mean understanding the relationship between a product and transportation costs. It might mean understanding the relationship between shelf space and sales. It might mean understanding the relationship between advertising and frequency of purchase. These and many other relationships comprise what are collectively referred to as competitive or business advantages. How advantageous a particular competitive advantage is depends upon the type of business in which you participate.

To develop a competitive advantage, two considerations need to be taken into account. The first consideration is perceiving that a relationship does indeed exist. Simply put, this means that if a business action is taken, some type of reaction (positive, it is hoped) will also occur. The second consideration is understanding the magnitude of the specific relationship. While a relationship may exist, it may hold little significance for a company. That is, for the investment required, the payoff will be relatively small.

Although it might be difficult to perceive a business relationship and assess its specific impact, the process a company must go through is relatively straightforward. The tricky part of competitive advantages for a company is that they are not always the same. The relationship that exists in one industry may have little or no impact in another. And even within an industry, the importance of a competitive advantage can change over time. If a company does not perceive the change as it is taking place, it can move swiftly from a position of top dog to being an underdog — and only realize too late what has taken place.

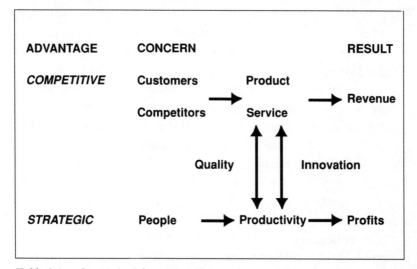

Table 9.1   Strategic Advantages Versus Competitive Advantages

Figure 9.1 illustrates the relationship between the two types of advantages. The first thing we need to recognize is that, while the primary focus differs for both, the two types of advantages are concerned with creating value through quality and innovation. Competitive advantages primarily involve increasing revenues while strategic advantages involve increasing productivity and profits.

Is a Profit Always Profitable?

Why is the preceding distinction between the types of advantages important? It is important because it forces us to look at the basic business from a different perspective. If we look at what is supposed to happen in a traditional organization, we interpret what is of interest to the company in the following manner:

$$Profits = Revenues - Costs$$

Profits occupy a central position, as they should. In a free market economy, for a business to survive and prosper, it must make a profit. How do we make profits? We try to create a competitive edge to increase our revenues, and usually our profits, in varying degrees, rise along with revenues. If we can't increase our revenues for some reason, what is left for a company to do? The answer most companies initially come to is "cut costs." Sometimes we use other terms such as "restructuring," but what it really means is to cut costs. Not that cutting costs is wrong. What is wrong is usually how it's done. What gets cut? Or, who gets cut?

Generally, the first things cut are people. Invariably, that means laying off workers. When the workers go, usually some managers go too. We then proceed down the line selling off buildings, machinery, property, and sometimes even whole businesses. In many instances, the cuts are made across the board without regard to how valuable the person or thing is or will be. While this certainly can boost profits, does it actually make the company better off? When we view profits in this way, we tend to get trapped into a roller coaster-like cycle of rising and declining profits. This sequence of events occurs because we get caught in what is referred to as a "zero-sum game" where gains in profits come at the expense of something else in the organization.

The preceding discussion presents one means of thinking about a company. There is, however, another equally valid way to view the profit relationship for a company. It takes the following form:

Profits = Revenues X Rate of Productivity

In its essence, this second formula for profits is the same as the first formula but our perspective has shifted. The second component of this second profit formula is not costs per se, as in the first formula, but what we are (or should be) truly interested in — "how effectively are we doing something." What we really are looking at still happens to include costs, but it is much more than merely costs. It is also related to what is accomplished from an overall organizational standpoint. What this relationship shows is that increased profits can come from keeping the same level of productivity, an implicit assumption made by many companies, but increasing revenues. Or increased profits can come from stable revenues, but an increasing productivity. With this viewpoint of profits, we can unbundle the all too prevalent revenue-cost notion so that each component part can stand alone, be viewed independently, and ultimately lead to maximizing profits.

Earlier in this section it was stated that the advantages caused companies to see things from a different perspective.

What does this mean? First, the two profit equations, while dealing with the same end point — profits — do so from distinctly different outlooks. The first equation basically views revenues and costs together; one has to balance the other to maintain stable levels of profitability. The organization becomes a necessary evil on the road to higher profits. If we have high growth, we sometimes try to ignore what is going on. If we have stable growth, we sometimes try to control what is going on. In far fewer instances do we try to use what is going on to our advantage. The second equation, in contrast, points out that the two components of the equation are separate questions to be answered. Returning to Figure 9.1, we see that the concerns in the second profit equation are different because each component deals with a different type of advantage.

There is, however, another change in perspective — one of attitude. What we also seem to observe is that when a company operates by the first equation, it seems to assume that growth in revenues is an external event (coming from growth in the economy or growth in the industry, and so forth). If we want to keep a constant level of profitability, the only way to make up for sagging revenues is to cut costs. What tends to happen in companies operating under the second equation is that once they realize they control their productivity, they also grasp that they have some control over their revenues. What seemed to be inevitable doesn't necessarily have to be inevitable. The ever present life cycle is a phenomenon that exists, but as Casio's imagination has shown, we don't have to live by what we think exists. Or, while the market is soft, we don't have to beat our breasts and gnash our teeth, as was shown earlier by the experience and reaction of Lincoln Electric to drastic drops in revenue. In other words, companies operating under the second equation seem to be innovative, respond to customer needs and so forth in a way that is fundamentally different from their competitors.

In the end, each component in the profit equation is a separate consideration regardless of how it is perceived. Being productive does not mean we will necessarily have high revenues. Likewise, being concerned with high revenues does not mean we will be doing it productively. High-flying companies always develop competitive advantages. Excellent companies always develop strategic advantages. Companies with sustained success always develop both.

The Missing 40 Percent

Throughout this book, the process leading to high levels of productivity has been discussed. We really have not put any numbers on high productivity thus far. How much can a company really expect to gain? Numbers such as 20 percent have already been presented in an earlier discussion. Is this a realistic or even reasonable expectation for most companies?

Although assessing potential productivity is difficult, we probably can develop some general rules of thumb. If we assume, in developing our organization, that productivity affects all functional areas similarly, we may be able to get a handle on what is and what is not possible. For example, what is happening at Lincoln Electric is fairly representative of what occurs in most other highly-productive organizations. The upper limit seems to be in the 70 to 80 percent range of what is actually possible (100 percent).

This range can be referred to as the real productivity or the average performance in high-productivity organizations. The difference between real productivity and maximum productivity is a function of the prevailing operating conditions and varies according to the existing circumstances. Operating conditions can be influenced by external causes. New laws, new technologies, and other events outside of the company sometimes bring unplanned problems as well as unplanned opportunities. Operating conditions also are influenced by internal causes. While people problems are minimized in productive companies, they are not completely eliminated. A company is still an organization composed of people with different needs and aspirations — it is not a utopia. While greater productivity rates can be achieved hypothetically, continued operation above the real level of productivity would result in only short-term benefits. Any gains over real productivity produced by sustained operations would come at the expense of long-run achievements.

Now, if we examine diverse companies such as Lincoln Electric, Nucor Steel, ServiceMaster, and other high performers, we see what might be termed a trend. The trend is that one measure of productivity — the sales per employee of these and other high performing companies — is generally at least twice the average of their respective industries. Thus, if we extrapolate what might be considered our best companies in terms of performance, we can produce a measure of productivity for average companies. Since the high-productivity companies in this book (and others not included) are operating by their own assessment between 70 and 80 percent of their maximum attainable productivity, average companies would appear to be operating in a 35 to 40-percent range of their maximum.

Where do average companies fit on the productivity growth curve? The description "average" is essentially a meaningless concept in this context, because average is a composite and really does not describe any particular company. Where do typical or ordinary companies that are not highly productive lie? Probably toward the bottom within a range just above or below the beginning position of the productivity growth curve. The more capable of the ordinary companies largely depend upon the activities of individual managers. Generally they have pockets of productivity and do somewhat better than their less effective counterparts who do not meet the lower level of the productivity growth curve.

Ordinary companies doing ordinary things tend to get mixed results. Sometimes things go well, sometimes poorly, but most of the time lackluster performance is tolerable as long as everyone else is in the same boat. With the costs that come to be expected as part of doing business (such as discipline, absenteeism, mediocre quality, lack of initiative and innovation), the typical company probably can expect an overall productivity rate of no better than 40 percent. For companies with less than "average" performance, the actual total productivity is probably 30 percent or less of their full potential. In any event, what we experience in absolute terms is a missing 40 percent (or more). In relative terms, this means that most companies probably can increase productivity by 100 percent, many companies probably can increase productivity by 200 percent, and some companies probably even can increase productivity by 300 percent or more!

The real significance of the missing 40 percent is that: (1) the consequences leading to high productivity seem to be uniform across manufacturing and service sector companies, and (2) the results can be observed in companies that are not in high-growth industries. Therefore, some of the confounding influences present when high-growth companies are observed are eliminated.

Today, technology has become inexorably linked with productivity. The great leaps in productivity that most companies desire can come only when the organization's technology and people merge. Technology, the perceived salvation of many companies, does not necessarily bring the levels of productivity it is capable of bringing because it is used to eliminate the perceived problem — people. This view of technology may in fact create new problems before, during, and after its implementation. In companies where employees experience a sense of ownership, people will not fight technology. They will assist in its implementation because they are not threatened.

The Last Reminder

During the course of our lifetime, it is likely that nearly all of us will be confronted by at least one truly startling and unforeseen environmental, social, economic, political, or technological change. It will not really be a trend as much as it will become a ground rule affecting the way we do things. Just as Corporate America's past successes were based on its ability to recognize and conform to the ground rules that came into existence, so future leadership will go to those companies best able to accommodate the new rules of the new game.

The new game is being formulated. The leaders have been the Japanese companies. As the report of the Public Agenda Foundation points out:

Although exchange rates are a factor, much of Japan's success has been due to its ability to marshall its human resources. According to one recent analysis, for example, Toyota has a $1718 cost advantage (after shipping) over General Motors in producing a small car. Some of this advantage is due to lower wages and fringe benefits ($550), and some is due to superior technology ($73). But about $1000 of the difference is attributable to skill in utilizing existing human resources. Japan's *skillful mobilization of the needs, abilities, and values of its work force dictates that America, if it wishes to be competitive, must utilize its human resources to the utmost.*

The "old" game rewarded those organizations that waited and reacted. The "new" game pays those that can understand, anticipate, and mobilize. To compete effectively in the new game, the company needs to have an understanding of how it views its organization. Is it merely an accumulation of skills or is it a group of people?

The companies and individuals that have been or will be successful are those that use their imagination. By at least one definition, imagination is simply the ability to see what is there. It does not really matter what Japan, West Germany, or any other country is doing. What does matter is how much imagination we have and how much imagination our organizations have. Millions of people use their imaginations each year to make resolutions for the New Year. The best news is that you do not have to wait until January 1 to find the missing 40 percent. When you make the 40-percent resolution, your new year starts as soon as you act on the resolution. To make the 40-percent resolution:

- Don't just sit in your office. Go out and say hello to people. If you have subordinates, talk to them about their jobs. Talk to your peers about your job. Talk to your superior about your job.
- Act with integrity. You will get credibility, trust, and respect up and down the organization.
- Live the vision. Remember the words of Marion Wade, founder of ServiceMaster, "If you don't live it, you don't believe it."

- Make sure you get what you need — but make doubly sure you provide others with what they need. Both are important!
- Ownership is usually defined in financial terms — people receive something because they have made an investment. Let's be sure we include everyone who makes an investment: those who get dividends, those who get interest payments, and those who get paychecks.

Epilogue

Epilogue

The difference between the notably successful institution and one whose record is simply run-of-the-mill is seldom very great. It does not consist of brilliant and inspired flashes of genius — certainly not over a considerable period of time. The difference rather is the small increment of extra performance diffused over a very large number of individuals at all levels of the organization.

> — Crawford H. Greenwalt
> former Chairman of the Board, E. I. DuPont

Each detail is important and success usually comes with attention to small details.

> — John Wooden
> Head Basketball Coach Emeritus, U.C.L.A.

*I*N America there is a close affinity between business and sports. The sports metaphor is used widely in day-to-day business activities. Businesses "draw up game plans" to deal with competitors or "get home run hitters" to help when times are tough. These and many other figurative phrases are commonly scattered through everyday conversations. Sports terms have come to be used widely because they describe quite pointedly and simply what is going on within a business.

In fact, sports organizations provide an undisguised model of how many of our businesses operate. When we examine companies, we get caught up in technology and innovation, asset manipulation, and other extraneous factors that certainly can be important to business success, but obscure what actually is going on within a firm that enables it to be successful over the longer term. The opening quotations on the making of a winning organization illustrate the commonality existing between business and sports.

If we assume that there are at least overt parallels between businesses and sports teams, the question becomes: Is any particular sport a better representation than another as a model for business? While all major American sports represent current businesses, Robert Keidel points out that basketball probably best represents the overall general development of business today — the post-industrial organization.

If we examine the sport of basketball, we see many steady winners: Bobby Knight of Indiana University, Dean Smith of the University of North Carolina, Denny Crum of the University of Louisville, Pat Reilly of the Los Angeles Lakers, and Red Auerbach of the Boston Celtics. However, the one coach who stands at the top in collegiate basketball and perhaps all of sports is John Wooden who coached at the University of California at Los Angeles (U.C.L.A.) from 1948 until his retirement in 1975. One writer comments, "Neither Knute Rockne, nor John McGraw, nor Connie Mack, nor Casey Stengel, nor Vince Lombardi, nor any other coach or manager has compiled anything close to the record of Wooden's teams."

What were John Wooden's accomplishments? The one for which he is probably most noted was winning ten national collegiate basketball championships in his last twelve years of coaching (seven of them in succession). In addition, during his collegiate coaching career he never had a losing season. While at U.C.L.A., he also had an 88-game winning streak (bridging four seasons), a 73-game winning streak, and twice had 40 or more game winning streaks. John Wooden's accomplishments have accorded him the honor of being classified not simply as a coach who can win but truly as a championship coach. In an era where back-to-back championships are the sign of a super team or super coaching, one can hardly find the words to describe the feat of John Wooden with ten championships in twelve years (especially at the collegiate level where currently nobody can play more than four years). What John Wooden accomplished obviously takes him out of the sphere of simply being an outstanding coach and into the realm of being an outstanding manager because of the organization and system he developed.

Wooden's Wisdom

What Makes a Champion?

I believe that John Wooden symbolizes the fact that being a championship-caliber organization is not a matter of luck, nor does it necessarily have to be an ephemeral quality. The first point is that there is a difference between simply being good or even very good and being of championship caliber. John Wooden notes, "The difference between a champion and a contender is slight." It should be noted that while a fine line distinguishes the champion from the contender, the difference is not inconsequential and certainly most difficult to perceive — let alone cross.

Questions to consider: Who are your competitors? The people in marketing, operations, finance, or the other companies?

Implication: The point of the preceding discussion is that it doesn't really matter how good the people are, or even how well they do what they are doing. What matters is what kind of team it is.

Importance of Team

John Wooden emphasized the concept of team no matter how talented the individuals were. The concept of team creates so much more than the sum of the individuals that John Wooden often proclaimed, "It's amazing what you can accomplish when you don't care who gets the credit." This is not to say that star players were under-utilized by John Wooden. Within the overall team framework, however, their strengths were magnified while the shortcomings of other team members were minimized. With this concept, not only could star players be stars but other players also could accomplish more than they might have otherwise. The truth of this philosophy is attested to by the fact that, "Not only did the [U.C.L.A.] Bruins win all those titles but 24 of their players eventually became first-team All Americans." A key to winning basketball for John Wooden was individual unselfishness. He recognized that only the team — not individuals — could win or lose. When individuals on the team are separated into winners and losers, the team always loses. As he was once told, "Individuals receive awards, teams win championships."

Questions to consider: Are some people more important than others in your company and treated like it?

Do people in your company feel that they are not quite as good as your competitors?

Implication: On John Wooden's teams, the term "team" was used quite loosely. Everyone who was responsible for the end result was part of the "team": the people who played in the game, the substitutes who got little or no playing time, the team managers and trainers — everyone involved received respect and recognition. On a championship team, everyone's efforts are recognized. The top performer does not lose anything, but everyone else gains. That is why championship teams are champions and it is the *difference* between good teams and champions. In developing a team concept, one shouldn't become blinded to what actually can be accomplished. Everyone, either as individuals or as organizations, has weaknesses. We cannot let the weaknesses, however, dictate the outcome. In fact, rather than viewing ourselves in terms of strengths and weaknesses, we should view our organizations in terms of their characteristics. The team then can be built around the existing characteristics.

Developing the Winning Team

The distinguishing factor about John Wooden's teams is that they did not play according to the other team's rules but played by their own standards. He observes, "I have no control over what they have but I have control over what I have." He comments further, "The more you become concerned with things over which you have no control, the less you are able to do those things that you are able to control." Therefore, based upon the people he had, John Wooden developed each team with its own unique style. While each team was unique, the underlying philosophy was that there was movement by design but not repetition. Each team played according to the U.C.L.A. script and each player knew the script but was not limited to playing a rigid role.

Was U.C.L.A. perfect? No, the team was emphatically not perfect. In fact, it made mistakes. John Wooden's position was that "the team that makes the most mistakes will usually win."

Questions to consider: Do people in your organization make mistakes? When mistakes are made what action is taken?

Implication: To be competitive, you play according to your competition; to be a championship team, you make the competition play by your rules. Sometimes you make mistakes as you make the rules but they are still rules that you have developed. The only way you can be prepared thoroughly and execute correctly is by knowing the rules. If the rules change according to each competitor, you can never be thoroughly prepared.

Learning Is Basic to Execution

John Wooden classified himself as a teacher and practice coach. He believed that championships are won in practice and executed during the game. Thus, a key part of winning was through learning. He further felt that the proper execution of fundamentals can become instinctive if taught properly. Thus, a major part of the learning was by repetition until things become automatic for the players. The team played the game naturally and only had to react when something unusual occurred. Through this process, John Wooden did not have to fire up a team emotionally before a game to have the team play well.

Question to consider: Does everyone in the organization know "what the organization is about" and what is to be accomplished?

Implication: Every manager is a teacher helping people learn about the fundamentals of their company. When people can execute what they are supposed to do, we don't need to fire up people — they fire up themselves. For every crisis where we try to gain extra productivity, a lull inevitably follows. Overall, the level of productivity tends to balance out. Only when we reach a higher plane can greater productivity be achieved.

Defining the Fine Line of Success

To one of the winningest coaches in basketball, success was not determined by the final score. John Wooden never talked about winning but emphasized to his players that they should always play as well as they could. Steve Patterson, a former U.C.L.A. player, comments on this philosophy: "The unique dynamic that Coach Wooden had was that he was genuinely able to accept less, to be satisfied with something other than perfection if he thought you were trying as hard as you could." In the final measure, John Wooden realized that only individuals themselves could determine whether they were successful — in life or playing a game.

While success is ultimately determined by the individual, the leader creates the focal point to assist individuals in their attainment of success. Perhaps, the ultimate compliment to John Wooden was provided by an opposing coach who said, "It doesn't pay to scout U.C.L.A. What they do is terribly predictable. The difficulty is, they do it so well."

The difference between the champion and the contender ultimately comes down to doing the basics right. What were the basics that made John Wooden teams unique? An observer described U.C.L.A. as "not only a team superbly skilled in the fundamentals, but a squad in equally superb physical condition." The observer goes on to describe one last point comprising the nucleus of success, "There is that other fetish, team play." With respect to the last point, team play, John Wooden takes an almost aesthetic perspective when he says, "I'm interested in teamwork; in the rhythm of the game; in the beauty of watching a play unfold that eventually leads to a basket." Thus, the simple formula of U.C.L.A.'s success was that the players knew the fundamentals, were able to execute the fundamentals, and did it together.

The hallmark of John Wooden teams is that while they didn't always have the best players, they always got the best out of the players they had. Which, as history has invariably shown, made them the best team. One example gives at least a partial glimpse of why they were best. In 1964, U.C.L.A. won its first championship with no player taller than 6' 5". Six members of that first championship team tried out for the 1964 Olympic team. One test given to all of the candidates measured the vertical jumping ability of an individual. The top four players were from U.C.L.A. In a tie for fifth were a U.C.L.A. player and an All-American player from another university. The seventh best player in terms of leaping ability was the last U.C.L.A. player, again tied with several other All-Americans. A key ingredient for U.C.L.A. players in being better than most of their competition was in being better prepared both mentally and physically.

In making his teams better prepared, John Wooden always took care of the details — large and small. What does a big-time coach do? What are the little things? John Wooden made sure that shoes fit his players' feet correctly, he made sure that his players put on their socks right, and he even taught them how to tie their shoelaces. Imagine that!

From the description thus far, one might assume that playing basketball was a hard, grueling experience at U.C.L.A. Hard maybe, but grueling, never. John Wooden also believed that players should enjoy what they were doing and even have some fun. He remarks, "We play a game the players enjoy to play and spectators enjoy to watch."

Questions to consider: Are the people working in the company well prepared? Are the people in the company doing their best? Are the people working in the company having fun?

Implications: The three basic factors considered for success in basketball certainly have parallels for business organizations. These are: (1) Train people so that they instinctively know what has to be done, (2) develop them so that they can perform effectively over the long haul, and most importantly, (3) everyone in a company should work like a team because that is what they are. The highest levels of achievement, ironically, come from paying attention to the smallest details. If all things large and small are attended to, the reality of the basic organizational values come to life and guide the actions of each individual. What do the managers pay attention to in your organization?

Further Observations on Managing

The preceding discussion focuses on the making of championship teams. It is also worthwhile to discuss briefly some general observations John Wooden has about managing. He emphatically emphasizes, "Don't make decisions on emotion or sympathy." He continues, "Emotion and sympathy are important qualities to have but are not the basis for making sound decisions." What did John Wooden think was important in dealing with people? He states, (1) make each person feel important, (2) make each person feel appreciated, (3) build each person up ("You don't build up the weak by tearing down the strong"), (4) *never* embarrass a person before their peers, and (5) don't compare one person to another.

Question to consider: The last question for a manager or a company to consider is one that John Wooden posed to his teams: "We are many, but are we much?"

Caveats

In the commentary on what he did as a coach, John Wooden also gave two sage bits of advice on what to watch out for. The first is "Don't mistake activity for achievement." He comments, "You need to have a product or it doesn't make any difference how many good players you have." The reason championship teams are champions is that they accomplish more than their competitors. The second bit of advice is "Failing to prepare is preparing to fail." This is especially important advice for programs or organizations that have been successful. The easiest thing to do is the same thing that brought success previously (the "if-it- ain't-broke-don't-fix-it" syndrome). For John Wooden, each basketball season was a completely new season. Past victories were to be savored and not imitated. Each year brought new challenges and new victories.

Art Imitating Reality?

The difference in any athletic event is the people. It is easy to see. What is more difficult to see is that it is exactly the same for businesses.

Some managers — like some coaches — try to get 110 or 120 percent from their people. John Wooden did not believe that people could give more than 100 percent. And, he is right. But what he did attempt to do was to get each individual to perform as closely to 100 percent as possible. Given that many organizations are only producing in the 30 to 40 percent range, the goal for these organizations should not be to get people to produce over their maximum but just to do their best.

References

References

CHAPTER 1

3   "Much of U.S. industry has," Tichy, Noel M. and Ulrich, David, "The Challenge of Revitalization," *New Management*, 2, 1985, p. 53. Reprinted by permission of John Wiley & Sons, Inc.

6   "You can't treat your customers," Block, Peter, *The Empowered Manager: Positive Political Skills at Work*, San Francisco, CA: Jossey-Bass Publishers, 1987, p. 112.

7   "The individual must," Rodgers, F. G. "Buck," *The IBM Way*, New York: Harper & Row, Publishers, 1986. p. 10.

7   "Big Japanese corporations treat," Tsurumi, Yoshi, "American Management Has Missed the Point. The Point is Management Itself," in *Quality, Productivity, and Competitive Position*, W. Edwards Deming, Cambridge, MA: Massachusetts Institute of Technology, Center for Advanced Engineering Study, 1982, p. 85.

8   "There was hardly a more," Peters Thomas J. and Waterman, Robert H. Jr., *In Search of Excellence*, New York: Harper & Row, 1980. p. 238–239.

8   "One *Excellence*-type slogan," Byrne, John A., "Business Fads: What's in-and out," *Business Week*, January 20, 1986, p. 60.

223

11 "The system of values," Boyle, Richard J., "Why wrestle with jellyfish?: Lessons in managing organizational change," *National Productivity Review*, Vol. 4, No. 2, Spring 1985, pp. 180–181. Reprinted with permission. Copyright 1985 by Executive Enterprises, Inc., 22 West 21st Street, New York, NY 10010-6904. All Rights Reserved

11 "The basic philosophy," Watson, Thomas J. Jr., *A Business and Its Beliefs: The Ideas That Helped Build IBM*, New York: McGraw-Hill Book Co., 1963. p. 5-6.

11 "The only sacred cow," Rodgers, F. G."Buck," *The IBM Way*, New York: Harper & Row, Publishers, 1986. p. 18.

12 "If the central beliefs," Davis, Stanley M., "Attempting major change? 10 pitfalls to avoid — and how," *Human Resource Planning*, 1984, p. 182.

12 "the leader's ability," Berlew, David E., "Leadership and Organizational Excitement," *California Management Review*, XVII, 1974, p. 5–37.

13 "Principles must," Rodgers, F. G."Buck," ibid., p. 10.

14 "most issues requiring," Sayles, L. R. and Wright, R. V. L., "The Use of Culture in Strategic Management," *Issues and Observations*, November 1985, p. 1.

15 "Purposes give a company," Pastin, Mark, *The Hard Problems of Management*, San Francisco, CA: Jossey-Bass Publishers, 1986, p. 152.

15 "Having no purpose," Pastin, Mark, ibid., p. 153.

16 "Virtually every action," Pastin, Mark, ibid., p. 153.

18 "Americans understand," Hall, Robert W., and Nakane, Jinichiro, "Developing Flexibility for Excellence in Manufacturing: Summary Results of a Japanese-American Study," *Target*, 4, 1988, p. 19.

18 "I always thought," Gaines, Sallie, "He Retired From Title, Not Power," *Chicago Tribune*, May 26, 1986, Sec. 4, p. 7. © Copyrighted, Chicago Tribune Company, all rights reserved, used with permission.

19 "We don't have to manage," Witt, Linda, "Coat of Family Philosophy Keeps Johnson Shining," *Chicago Tribune*, November 18, 1985, Sec. 4, p. 6.

19 "The most successful large corporations," Ohmae, Kenichi, *The Mind of the Strategist*, New York: McGraw-Hill Book Co., 1982, p. 207.

20 "Nearly one half," Yankelovich, Daniel, and Immerwahr, John, *Putting the Work Ethic to Work*, New York: The Public Agenda Foundation, 1983, p. 25.

20 "Management doesn't," Yankelovich, Daniel, and Immerwahr, John, *Putting the Work Ethic to Work*, New York: The Public Agenda Foundation, 1983, p. 28.

21 "We were deeply impressed," Naisbitt, John and Aburdene, Patricia, *Re-inventing the Corporation*, New York: Warner Books, 1985. p. 256.

21 "One of the best kept," Naisbitt, John and Aburdene, Patricia ibid., p. 256.

CHAPTER 2

46 "Statistically we," Rhodes, Lucien, "The Passion of Robert Swiggett," Reprinted with permission, *Inc.*, (June, 1984). Copyright © 1984 by Goldhirsh Group, Inc., 38 Commerical Wharf, Boston, MA 02110. p. 126.

46 "People like to play," Rhodes, Lucien, ibid., p. 132.

48 "there are no," *The Development of Kollmorgen,* A speech by Robert L. Swiggett, President and Chief Executive, © Innovation Associates, 1981. p. 5.

48 "The only way," Rhodes, Lucien, ibid., p. 134.

49 "Few people have," *The Development of Kollmorgen*, A speech by Robert L. Swiggett, President and Chief Executive, © Innovation Associates, 1981. p. 10.

49 "Look at the," *The Development of Kollmorgen*, A speech by Robert L. Swiggett, President and Chief Executive, © Innovation Associates, 1981. p. 13.

50 "People lie," Rhodes, Lucien, ibid., p. 140.

53 "We perceive profitable," "ServiceMaster: The Protestant ethic helps clean hospitals better," *Business Week*, February 19, 1979, p. 58.

54 "Our willingness," Wessner, Kenneth T., "A Company Needs Vision as well as Controls," Reprinted, by permission of publisher, from *Management Review*, August 1981, © 1981, American Management Association, New York. All rights reserved. p. 35.

67   "The concept of," Grundstrom, William G., "Motorola: Striving for Innovation," *Forum Issues 9*, Spring 1988, p. 1. Copyright © 1988 by the Forum Corporation. Reprinted with permission.

67   "Motorola was," Grundstrom, William G., "Motorola: Striving for Innovation," *Forum Issues 9*, Spring 1988, p. 2. Copyright © 1988 by the Forum Corporation. Reprinted with permission.

CHAPTER 3

72   "no culture exists," Hirsch, Jr., E. D., "Cultural Literacy," Reprinted from *The American Scholar*, Volume 52, No. 2, Spring 1983, Copyright © 1983 by the author, with the permission of the publisher, the Phi Beta Kappa Society. p. 167.

CHAPTER 4

93   *In fact*, See the following for further discussion: Peters, Tom and Austin, Nancy, *A Passion for Excellence*, New York: Random House, 1985.

96   "employees can handle," Nelton, Sharon, "Motivating for Success," *Nation's Business*, 76, 1988, p. 26.

101 "In 1965," Peters, Tom, "On Excellence," *Chicago Tribune*, Sec. 4, November 17, 1986, p. 26.

102 *Current research*, See the following for further discussion: Drehmer, David E. and Grossman, Jack H., "Scaling

Managerial Respect: A Developmental Perspective," *Educational and Psychological Measurement*, 44, 1984, pp. 763–767.

103 "It's not so much," "Managing cause and effect," *Productivity Newsletter*, 8, 1987, p. 3.

104 "Some actions," *Productivity Newsletter*, ibid. pp. 4-5.

CHAPTER 5

111 "22 percent of them," "New study finds high level of cynicism among U.S. and European workforces," *International Management*, 40, 1985, p. 76.

112 "begins to more fully," Ket de Vries, Manfred F. R. and Miller, Danny, *The Neurotic Organization*, San Francisco CA: Jossey-Bass, 1984, p. 122.

114 "Suppose a groundskeeper," _____, "ServiceMaster brings invisible employees to light," Copyrighted material reprinted with permission of *Employee Relations and Human Resources Bulletin*, No. 1668, (interview with Ken Fisher, Director for People Development, for ServiceMaster Limited Partnership, Downers Grove, IL). Bureau of Business Practice, 24 Rope Ferry Road, Waterford, CT 06386. July 21, 1988, Section 1. p. 2.

114 *Organizational researcher*, See the following for further discussion: Komacki, Judith L., "Toward Effective Supervision: An Operant Analysis and Comparison of Managers at Work," *Journal of Applied Psychology*, 71, 1986, pp. 270–278.

115 "give the people," Nelton, Sharon, ibid., p. 24.

118 "to put into words," Block, Peter, ibid, p. 83.

119 "The hardest thing," Rodgers, Buck, "Thoughts on the Well-Run Organization," *Forum Issues 7*, Spring 1987, p. 12. Copyright © 1987 by The Forum Corporation. Reprinted with permission.

123 "First, if you," Kuzmits, Frank and Sussman, Lyle, "Credibility Is a Way to Overcome Imperfection," *Louisville Courier-Journal*, April 7, 1986, Sec. C, p. 2.

126 "Although work behaviors," Yankelovich, Daniel and Immerwahr, John, ibid., p. 4.

126 "Good people," Cattabiani, E. J., and White, R. P., "Participative Management," *Issues and Observations*, August 1983, p. 2.

126 "The lack of trust," Diffie-Couch, Dr. Priscilla, "Building a feeling of trust in the company," Reprinted, by permission of publisher, from *Supervisory Management*, April 1984, © 1984. American Management Association, New York. All rights reserved. p. 34.

CHAPTER 6

132 "Vision is," Fritz, Robert, *The Path of Least Resistance*, New York: Ballantine, 1989. p. 70.

135 *In his Emmy*, See *Creativity with Bill Moyers*, New York: The Corporation for Entertainment and Learning, 1981.

135 "One reason," *The Path of Least Resistance*, New York: Ballantine, 1989. p. 60.

135 "What is actually," Fritz, Robert, ibid, p. 62.

136 "every year," Fritz, Robert, ibid, p. 61.

137 "companies who create," Tichy, Noel M. and Ulrich, David ibid., p. 56.

140 "it would be," Willbur, Jerald L., *Mentoring and Achievement Motivation as Predictors of Career Success*, Ed.D. Dissertation, Northern Illinois University, 1986. p. 127.

140 "both mentors," ibid, pp. 149–150.

140 *When learning is,* See the following for further discussion: Belohlav, J., Raho, L. and Fiedler, K., "Assimilating new technology into the organization: An assessment of McFarlan and McKenney's model," *MIS Quarterly*, 11, 1987, 47–57.

141 *These degrees of,* See the following for further discussion: (1) Kelman, H. C., "Compliance, identification, and internalization: Three processes of attitude change," *Journal of Conflict Resolution*, 2, 1958, 51–60. (2) O'Reilly, Charles R. and Chatman, Jennifer, "Organizational Commitment and Psychological Attachment: The Effects of Compliance, Identification, and Internalization on Prosocial Behavior," *Journal of Applied Psychology*, 71, 1986, 492–499.

143 *With internalization,* See the following for further discussion: (1) Mowday, Richard T., Steers, Richard M., and

Porter, Lyman W., "The Measurement of Organizational Commitment," *Journal of Vocational Behavior*, 14, 1979, 224–247. (2) Sheldon, M. E., "Investments and Involvements as Mechanisms Producing Commitment to the Organization," *Administrative Science Quarterly*, 16, 1971, 142–150. (3) Mowday, Richard T., Porter, Lyman W., and Steers, Richard M., *Employee-Organizational Linkages*, New York: Academic Press, 1982.

144 *In fact*, See the following for further discussion: (1) Zahara, Shaker, A., "Understanding Organizational Commitment," *Supervisory Management*, 1984, 16–20. (2) Meyer, John P. and Allen, Natalie J., "Links between work experiences and organizational commitment during the first year of employment: A longitudinal analysis," *Journal of Occupational Psychology*, 61, 1988, 195–209.

CHAPTER 7

149 *Some research studies*, See the following for further discussion: (1) Deci, E. "The effects of externally mediated rewards on intrinsic motivation," *Journal of Personality and Social Psychology*, 18, 1971, 105–115. (2) Deci, E. "The effects of contingent and non-contingent rewards and controls on intrinsic motivation," *Organizational Behavior and Human Performance*, 8, 1972, 217–229. (3) Deci, E. *Intrinsic Motivation*, New York: Plenum Publishing Co., 1975. (4) Arnold, H., "Effects of performance feedback and extrinsic reward upon high extrinsic motivation, 17, 1976, 275–288. (5) Farr, J., Vance, R., McIntyre, R., "Further examinations of the relationship between reward contingency and motivation, 20, 1977, 31–53.

149 *However, it has,* See the following for further discussion: Ross, M., "The self-perception of intrinsic motivation," In J. Harvey, W. Ickes, and R. Kidd (Eds.) *New Directions in Attribution Research*, Vol. 1, Hillsdale, NJ: Lawrence Erlbaum Associates, 1976.

150 "we're talking about human beings," Sugarman, Aaron, "Success Through People," *Incentive*, 162, 1988, p. 28.

151 "one of the most," Yankelovich, Daniel and Immerwahr, John, ibid., p. 26.

152 "First, employees may," Sashkin, Marshall, "Participative Management Is an Ethical Imperative," Reprinted, by permission of publisher, from *Organizational Dynamics*, Spring 1984. © 1984 American Management Association, New York. All rights reserved. p. 5.

CHAPTER 8

169 "The employee gives," Grant, Philip C., "Rewards: The Pizzazz Is the Package, Not the Prize," *Personnel Journal*, 67, 1988, p. 76.

178 Transformations, Information in this section was obtained from the following: "People Power Drives Cheboygan's Business," *Moonbeams*, 49, June 1988, pp. 4–8, and discussions with management.

180 "the organization itself," _____, "People Power Drives Cheboygan's Business," *Moonbeams*, 49, June 1988, p. 5.

181 "for years tremendous," *Moonbeams*, ibid., p. 5.

182 *More and More,* Information in this section was obtained from the following: Hall, Robert W., "Volunteers in Action Digital Equipment Corporation—Albuquerque," *Target,* 4, 1988, pp. 24–27 and discussions with management.

183 *Not just manufacturing,* Information in this section was obtained from the following: Jewell, Donald O. and Jewell, Sandra, F., "An Example of Economic Gainsharing in the Restaurant Industry," *National Productivity Review,* Spring 1987, 6, pp. 134–143.

CHAPTER 9

198 *This competitive edge,* See the following for further discussion: (1) Porter, Michael E., *Competitive Advantage,* New York: The Free Press, 1985. (2) Belohlav, J. and Giddens-Emig K., "Selecting a master strategy," *Journal of Business Strategy,* 8, 1987, pp. 76–82. (3) Carroll, P., "The link between performance and strategy," *Journal of Business Strategy,* 2, 1982, pp. 3–20.

202 *The ever present life cycle,* For a further discussion of Casio see: Ohmae, Kenichi, *The Mind of the Strategist,* McGraw-Hill Book Co. 1982.

206 "Although exchange rates," Yankelovich, Daniel, and Immerwahr, John, ibid., p. 4.

EPILOGUE

212 *Robert Keidel points out,* For an interesting discussion on the parallels between sports teams and business organizations see: Keidel, Robert W., "Baseball, football, and bas-

ketball: Models for business," *Organizational Dynamics*, Winter 1984, pp. 5–18.

212 "Neither Knute Rockne," Hano, Arnold, "Winning with nice guys and a pyramid of principles," *The New York Times Magazine*, December 2, 1973, p. 134. "Copyright © 1973 by the New York Times Company. Reprinted by permission."

214 "It's amazing what," Myslenski, Skip, "On College Basketball," March 22, 1990, Sec. 4, p. 8. © Copyright, Chicago Tribune Company. All rights reserved, used with permission.

214 "Not only did," Elderkin, Phil, "John Wooden's view from retirement on basketball, discipline," March 12, 1986, p. 20. Excerpts reprinted by permission from *Christian Science Monitor*, © 1986 The Christian Science Publishing Society. All rights reserved.

215 "The more you become," Capouya, John, "John Wooden," *Sport*, 77, December 1986, p. 51.

215 "The team that makes," Capouya, John, "John Wooden," *Sport*, 77, December 1986, p. 140.

217 "the unique dynamic," Capouya, John, "John Wooden," *Sport*, 77, December 1986, p. 51.

217 "It doesn't pay," Hano, Arnold, "Winning with nice guys and a pyramid of principles," *The New York Times Magazine*, December 2, 1973, p. 138. "Copyright © 1973 by the New York Times Company. Reprinted by permission."

217 "not only a team," Hano, Arnold, "Winning with nice guys and a pyramid of principles," *The New York Times Magazine*, December 2, 1973, p. 142. "Copyright © 1973 by the New York Times Company. Reprinted by permission."

217 "there is that," Hano, Arnold, "Winning with nice guys and a pyramid of principles," *The New York Times Magazine*, December 2, 1973, p. 143. "Copyright © 1973 by the New York Times Company. Reprinted by permission."

217 "I'm interested in teamwork," Elderkin, Phil, "John Wooden's view from retirement on basketball, discipline," Excerpts reprinted by permission from *Christian Science Monitor*, © 1986 The Christian Science Publishing Society, All rights reserved, March 12, 1986, p. 20.

218 "We play a game," Hano, Arnold, "Winning with nice guys and a pyramid of principles," *The New York Times Magazine*, December 2, 1973, p. 138. "Copyright © 1973 by the New York Times Company. Reprinted by permission."

220 "Failing to prepare," Capouya, John, "John Wooden," *Sport*, 77, December 1986, p. 140.

About the Author

A graduate of the University of Cincinnati, James Belohlav is currently Associate Professor of Management at DePaul University. He is also accredited by several professional organizations, including the American Society for Personnel Administration as a Professional in Human Resources, and the National Management Association as a Certified Manager. He has played an active role in community affairs as consultant to the cities of West Carrollton and Englewood, Ohio, and the Montgomery County Government in Dayton, Ohio. He served as Commissioner and Vice-Chairman to the Police and Fire Commission in Mt. Prospect, Illinois, and as expert advisor on the Public Employee Substance Abuse Impact Panel for the State of Ohio.

The author of over 30 published articles on management and management information systems, he wrote *The Art of Disciplining Your Employees* published by Prentice-Hall in 1985. He is a member of the Academy of Management, the Decision Sciences Institute, and the American Association for Artificial Intelligence and has participated in educational development activities with Ford Aerospace and Communications Corporation, Merchants National Bank in Muncie, Indiana, Ball Corporation, the United States Air Force, and the Independent Banker's Association.

He resides in Mt. Prospect, Illinois, with his wife and two children.

Index

A

Aburdene, Patricia, 21
ACE, 182-183
achievement, 105-106, 220
acquisitions, 16, 17, 26
actions of successful companies, 73-88, 125-127
activity
    boards, 43
    vs. achievement, 220
Advanced Certification Board, 45
advantage, competitive, 196-200
advisory board, management, 30
aerosol, 77
alienation, 111-112, 126
All Committed to Excellence (ACE), 182-183
American Express, 150
Anderson, Dick, 56
Attends underpad, 181
attention, paying, 93-95, 113-117, 127, 151-152
Austin, Nancy, 83

B

Balc, Alexander, 54
Baseler, Dave, 51, 70
basketball, 212
Beecher, Henry Ward, 147
belonging, sense of, 93-95, 112-113
Best Foods Company, 39-45, 75-76, 78
Bills, Daniel, 103, 104
blame, fixing the , 187
Block, Peter, 118-119
bonus, 50, 66, 115

Brooks, Ron, 93, 182
Bruins (U.C.L.A.), 214
Burns, Dick, 180

C

case-packing machine, 181
Cash, Tom, 150
Casio, 202
"Camelot phenomena," 136
Cattabiani, E.J., 126
caveats, 87-88
CEOs, 86-87
challenge on the job, 21
champion, qualities of a, 213
change, 98-100, 152
"checkbook owner" concept, 180
Christian ethics, 29
Clark Equipment Company, 175-178
Comer, Gary, 60, 87
commitment, 100-102, 141-144
    building, 92
    organizational, 19-22, 64-65, 143
    worker, 191
committees, operating, 44-45
communication, 43, 62, 64-66, 84-85, 175-177, 180, 201
    employee meetings, 37, 39
    programs, 37
compensation
    Lincoln Electric Co., 31
    system of, 148-151
competition, 29, 80, 122
competitive advantage, 198-200
compliance, 141
confidence, generating, 91, 95-96, 102, 118-123

conflict, 166
contribution, 93-95
control, 74, 83, 87, 106, 215
coordinator role, 44
costs, cutting, 200-202
councils, 43
Cowan, Keith, 31
CPC International, 42
credibility, 95, 122-123, 126-127
customer, 29
culture
    corporate, 97
    of our society, 94

D

daycare program, 36
Dean's List, 26-27
decision making, 152, 219
Delta Airline, 132
Deming, W. Edwards, 81
destiny, creating your, 131, 144
deterioration of organizations,
    symptoms of, 17-18
development of people, 19. See also
    people
Digital Electronics Corporation, 93,
    182-183
direction, 92, 98-100, 102, 137-140,
    144
DuPont, E.I., 211

E

E.I. DuPont, 211
education, 77-79
    Motorola, 67-76
800 telephone number, 77

employee communications
    meetings, 37, 39
end result of work, 21
ethics, 29, 126
evaluation of employees, 32-33
excellence, 77
execution, learning and, 216
expectations, negative, 131

F

failure, 91-92
fast-food business, 183-186
fear, 81
feedback, 95-96, 127
financial equity, 79
Fisher, Ken, 114
fit, organizational, 92, 97-98, 102,
    131, 144
fitness center, company, 36
flexibility, 74
focusing, 98-100
Fortune 500 companies, 27
Franklin, Benjamin, 91
Fritz, Robert, 135-136
Fuller, Thomas, 195

G

gain-sharing program, 43, 175-178,
    184-186
Galvin, Bob, 62, 148
General Motors, 206
goals, setting, 152
Granville-Phillips Company, 103-
    104
Great Britain, 79
Green Bay Packers, 95
Greenwalt, Crawford H., 211

grieving process, 187
growth, rapid, 26
Grundstrom, William, 66-67

H

Hacquebord, Heero, 189
Hargreaves, Bill, 53
Harvard Business School, 46
honesty. See integrity
human resource management, 53
human scale, 85-86

I

"I Recommend" process, 66
IBM, 78, 190
identification, 141
"if-it-ain't-broke-don't-fix-it"
    syndrome, 220
Immerwahr, John, 191
implementation of new system, 188,
    190
incentive management system, 29
individual and his job, case study,
    170-174
information-sharing, 84
innovation, 187-189
integration, individual, 131
integrity, 95, 118-119, 207
internal development of people, 19.
    See also people
internalization, 14-143
inventory
    Just-In-Time (JIT), 18, 192
    on-time delivery of, 28

J

Japanese business, 18, 21, 79, 186,
    192, 206-207
Jewel Companies, 18
Jewell, Donald O., 185
Jewell, Sandra F., 185
JIT, 18
job enrollment program, 60
job security. See security, job
jobs, 18-84
Johnson, H.F., Sr., 35
Johnson, Sam, 19, 39
Johnson, S.C., 77
Johnson, S.C., and Son, Inc., 34-39
Johnson, S.J., Company, 19
Johnson Wax, 34
Johnson Wax Weekly, 37
Just Ask program, The, 37, 38
Just-In-Time (JIT) inventory
    method, 18, 192
justification, concern with, 18

K

kanban, 28
Keidel, Robert, 212
Kets de Vries, Manfred, 112
Keys to Success, Motorola, 62-63
Kollmorgen Corporation, 45-51
"Kolture workshops," 48
Komacki, Judi, 114-115
Kuzmits, Frank, 123

L

Lands' End, 56-63, 77, 87
learning, commitment to, 139-140,
    216

lessons, 25-70
Lincoln, James F., 29
Lincoln, John C., 29
Lincoln Electric, 27-34, 75-78, 133-
    135, 148, 150-151, 190, 192,
202, 203-204
listening, 121-122
Lombardi, Vince, 95
Longfellow, Henry Wadsworth, 110
Lowell, James Russell, 73
loyalty, 100-101

M

machine, case packing, 181
mail order company, 56
management-development
    programs, 19
management
    education, 79
    human resource, 53-54
    observation of workers, 114-115
    participative, 75-76
    Motorola, 64-67
    perspective, 25-26
    principles, 42-43
    strategic, 195-220
    style, 76
    system incentive, 29
    top, 86-87
Management Advisory Board, 75
Management By Walking Around
    (MBWA), 116
Management Council, 45
manager's story, one, 123-125
managing, John Wooden's
    comments on, 219-220
MBWA, 116
McDonald's, 184

Megatrends, 21
mentors, 140
mergers, 16, 17, 26
merit rating, 30-33
Miller, Danny, 112
Mitsubishi, 27
model for high performance, 102-
    106
money, 148-151
    productivity and, 149-150
morale, 36
motivation, 21, 28, 62, 149
Motorola, Inc., 62-70, 77, 138, 148,
    174
Moyers, Bill, 135
Mulhollen, Roger, 36
mutuality
    establishment of, 144
    of perspective, 169-170

N

Naisbitt, John, 21
neurotic organizations, 112-113
News Tabloid, 60
newspaper, in-house, 37, 60
Nucor Steel, 204
numbers, 18, 93-94

O

objectives, 175
Ohmae, Ken, 19
Olympic team, 1964, 218
One-Minute Manager, 116
onion patch strategy, 188, 189
openness, 96

operating committees, Best Foods, 44-45
operating system, Best Foods, 43-45
organizational illiteracy, 78
organizations, neurotic, 112-113
orientations, establishment of initial, 131
ownership, sense of, 141-144, 174, 208

P-Q

package inserts, Lands' End, 60-61
Pampers, 178-182
paradoxes, management, 73-74
participation, management, 64-65, 75-76, 151-154
participative management, 75-76
Participative Management Process (PMP), 64
Passion for Excellence, A, 93
Patterson, Steve, 217
Pastin, Mark, 83, 86
payouts, 176-178
Pearson, Sally, 187
people, development of, 17, 19, 29, 77-79, 197
Pepper, John, 119
performance, defining high, 90-106
    indicators, 176
    investment in high, 111-128
    model for high, 102-105
    of workers, 20-22
    principles for high, 75-87
    realities of high, 105-106
    stimulating quality, 191
Perkins, Donald, S., 18
Peters, Tom, 93
philosophy, Kollmorgen, 47

Plant Review Board, 45
PMP, 64
position information, 41
pride, point of, 76-77
principles, 29
    of basic management, 42-43
    for high performance, 75-87
Principles of Doing Business, Lands' End, 57
problems
    in high productivity work systems, 147-166
    solving, 152
Procter & Gamble, 119-121, 142, 178-182, 187
production, Best Foods, 43-44
productivity, 20-22, 169-170, 201-202
    gain-sharing program, 175-178
    growth curve, 203-205
    job security and, 81-82
    Lincoln Electric Co., 27-34
    money and, 149-150
    reality of, 80
profits, 200-203
program, management-development, 19
promises, 118
promotion, tenure-based, 19
Public Agency Foundation, 20, 22, 126, 151, 206
purpose, 132
quality, 56-60

R

reactions, 125-127
raises, 21

reality
    confronting, 135-136
    rules, 80-81
recognition, 30, 92, 93-95, 102, 151-152
refocusing, 187
respect, mutual, 153
resistance to new systems, 186-187
responsibility, 30, 31, 34, 83, 87
    paradox of, 74
"The Rest Is Shadow," 35
restaurant business, 183-186
results, 81
retirement, 26, 31, 50
revenues, 200
rewards, 30-31, 79-80, 148-151, 169-170, 175-178
Rogers, Buck, 119

S

salaries, 44
satisfaction, job, 112
Scholtes, Peter, R., 189
security, 30, 31
    job, 19, 62, 81-82
self-defeating success, paradox of, 74
self-esteem, 48, 49, 79, 113, 114
self-fulfilling prophecy, 106
self-interest, 20, 144
service, 56-60
ServiceMaster Company, 51-55, 114, 138, 139, 148-149, 204, 207
Shearon, Larry, 42, 45
simplicity, 29
Skippy peanut butter, 40
Smithsonian Institution, 178

Social System Support Task Force, 44-45
sports, business and , 211-220
status quo, 187-188
stickers, 125
strategic
    advantage, 196-198
    first step, 17-20
    management, 195-220
strike, 179
success
    defining fine line of, 217-219
    factors in organizations, 19
    paradox of self-defeating, 74
suggestion box, 101
support, 95-96, 122, 127
Sussman, Lyle, 123
Sutherland, Jr., Duncan B., 131
Swiggett, Jim, 46
Swiggett, Robert, 46, 47, 48, 49, 50-51

T

teams, work, 43-44
technical expertise, 137, 197-198
technician work system, 179-180
techniques, preoccupation with, 18
technology, productivity and, 205-206
team
    importance of, 214-215
    developing the winning, 215-216
telephone operators, 59-60
tenure-based promotion, 19
Thoreau, Henry David, 169
time, discretionary, 133-134
Toyota, 101, 206

training, 67-70, 219
trust, 48, 64-66, 95, 126-127, 153

U-V

uncertainty, 186-187
University of California at Los
   Angeles, 212
vacations, 28
values
   corporate, 138
   creation of, 196
VIA, 182-183
vision, organizational, 97-98, 131-
   137, 207
Volunteers In Action (VIA), 182-183

W

Wade, Marion, 51, 207
Wal-Mart Stores, 87

Walton, Sam, 87
Wessner, Ken, 51
West Germany, 79
Westinghouse, 126
Wilbur, Jerry, 140
winnings, everyone gets part of the,
   79-80
Wooden, John, 211-220
work ethic, 126
work hours, decreasing, 28
work teams, 43-44
workers
   commitment, 191
   performance of, 20-22
Wright, Frank Lloyd, 34

X-Y-Z

Yankelovich, Daniel, 191
Youngblood, Jack, 48, 50
"zero-sum game," 201

The Eternal Venture Spirit
An Executive's Practical Philosophy
by Kazuma Tateisi

Like human health, organizational health depends on discovering the causes of symptoms that indicate an imbalance in the system. Tateisi, founder and CEO of Omron Industries, one of Japan's leading electronics companies, analyzes the signals of "big business disease" and how to respond to them so that technological innovation and entrepreneurial spirit can thrive as the organization grows and the market changes. An outstanding book on long-term strategic management.
ISBN 0-915299-55-0 / 176 pages / $19.95 / Order code EVS-BK

Manager Revolution!
A Guide to Survival in Today's Changing Workplace
by Yoshio Hatakeyama

An extraordinary blueprint for effective management, here is a step-by-step guide to improving your skills, both in everyday performance and in long-term planning. *Manager Revolution!* explores in detail the basics of the Japanese success story and proves that it is readily transferable to other settings. Written by the president of the Japan Management Association and a bestseller in Japan, here is a survival kit for beginning and seasoned managers alike. Each chapter includes case studies, checklists, and self-tests.
ISBN 0-915299-10-0 / 208 pages / $24.95 / Order code MREV-BK

Better Makes Us Best
by John Psarouthakis

A short, engaging, but powerful and highly practical guide to performance improvement for any business or individual. Focusing on incremental progress toward clear goals is the key; you become "better" day by day. It's a realistic, personally fulfilling, action-oriented, and dynamic philosophy that has made Psarouthakis's own company a member of the Fortune 500 in just ten years. Buy a copy for everyone in your work force, and let it work for you.
ISBN 0-915299-56-9 / 112 pages / $16.95 / Order code BMUB-BK

COMPLETE LIST OF TITLES FROM PRODUCTIVITY PRESS

Akao, Yoji (ed.). **Quality Function Deployment: Integrating Customer Requirements into Product Design**
ISBN 0-915299-41-0 / 1990 / 387 pages / $ 75.00 / order code QFD

Asaka, Tetsuichi and Kazuo Ozeki (eds.). **Handbook of Quality Tools: The Japanese Approach**
ISBN 0-915299-45-3 / 1990 / 336 pages / $59.95 / order code HQT

Belohlav, James A. **Championship Management: An Action Model for High Performance**
ISBN 0-915299-76-3 / 1990 / 265 pages / $29.95 / order code CHAMPS

Birkholz, Charles and Jim Villella. **The Battle to Stay Competitive: Changing the Traditional Workplace**
ISBN 0-915-299-96-8 / 1991 / 110 pages / $9.95 /order code BATTLE

Christopher, William F. **Productivity Measurement Handbook**
ISBN 0-915299-05-4 / 1985 / 680 pages / $137.95 / order code PMH

D'Egidio, Franco. **The Service Era: Leadership in a Global Environment**
ISBN 0-915299-68-2 / 1990 / 165 pages / $29.95 / order code SERA

Ford, Henry. **Today and Tomorrow**
ISBN 0-915299-36-4 / 1988 / 286 pages / $24.95 / order code FORD

Fukuda, Ryuji. **CEDAC: A Tool for Continuous Systematic Improvement**
ISBN 0-915299-26-7 / 1990 / 144 pages / $49.95 / order code CEDAC

Fukuda, Ryuji. **Managerial Engineering: Techniques for Improving Quality and Productivity in the Workplace** (rev.)
ISBN 0-915299-09-7 / 1986 / 208 pages / $39.95 / order code ME

Grief, Michel. **The Visual Factory: Building Participation Through Shared Information**
ISBN 0-915299-67-4 / 1991 / 320 pages / $49.95 / order code VFAC

Hatakeyama, Yoshio. **Manager Revolution! A Guide to Survival in Today's Changing Workplace**
ISBN 0-915299-10-0 / 1986 / 208 pages / $24.95 / order code MREV

Hirano, Hiroyuki. **JIT Factory Revolution: A Pictorial Guide to Factory Design of the Future**
ISBN 0-915299-44-5 / 1989 / 227 pages / $49.95 / order code JITFAC

Hirano, Hiroyuki. **JIT Implementation Manual: The Complete Guide to Just-In-Time Manufacturing**
ISBN 0-915299-66-6 / 1990 / 1006 pages / $2500.00 / order code HIRANO

Horovitz, Jacques. **Winning Ways: Achieving Zero-Defect Service**
ISBN 0-915299-78-X / 1990 / 165 pages / $24.95 / order code WWAYS

Japan Human Relations Association (ed.). **The Idea Book: Improvement Through TEI (Total Employee Involvement)**
ISBN 0-915299-22-4 / 1988 / 232 pages / $49.95 / order code IDEA

Japan Human Relations Association (ed.). **The Service Industry Idea Book: Employee Involvement in Retail and Office Improvement**
ISBN 0-915299-65-8 / 1990 / 294 pages / $49.95 / order code SIDEA

Productivity Press, Inc., Dept. BK, P.O. Box 3007, Cambridge, MA 02140 1-800-274-9911

Japan Management Association (ed.). **Kanban and Just-In-Time at Toyota: Management Begins at the Workplace** (rev.), Translated by David J. Lu
ISBN 0-915299-48-8 / 1989 / 224 pages / $36.50 / order code KAN

Japan Management Association and Constance E. Dyer. **The Canon Production System: Creative Involvement of the Total Workforce**
ISBN 0-915299-06-2 / 1987 / 251 pages / $36.95 / order code CAN

Jones, Karen (ed.). **The Best of TEI: Current Perspectives on Total Employee Involvement**
ISBN 0-915299-63-1 / 1989 / 502 pages / $175.00 / order code TEI

JUSE. **TQC Solutions: The 14-Step Process**
ISBN 0-915299-79-8 / 1991 / 416 pages / 2 volumes / $120.00 / order code TQCS

Kanatsu, Takashi. **TQC for Accounting: A New Role in Companywide Improvement**
ISBN 0-915299-73-9 / 1991 / 244 pages / $45.00 / order code TQCA

Karatsu, Hajime. **Tough Words For American Industry**
ISBN 0-915299-25-9 / 1988 / 178 pages / $24.95 / order code TOUGH

Karatsu, Hajime. **TQC Wisdom of Japan: Managing for Total Quality Control**, Translated by David J. Lu
ISBN 0-915299-18-6 / 1988 / 136 pages / $34.95 / order code WISD

Kaydos, Will. **Measuring, Managing, and Maximizing Performance**
ISBN 0-915299- 98-4 / 1991 / 208 pages / $34.95 / order code MMMP

Kobayashi, Iwao. **20 Keys to Workplace Improvement**
ISBN 0-915299-61-5 / 1990 / 264 pages / $34.95 / order code 20KEYS

Lu, David J. **Inside Corporate Japan: The Art of Fumble-Free Management**
ISBN 0-915299-16-X / 1987 / 278 pages / $24.95 / order code ICJ

Merli, Giorgio. **Total Manufacturing Management: Production Organization for the 1990s**
ISBN 0-915299-58-5 / 1990 / 224 pages / $39.95 / order code TMM

Mizuno, Shigeru (ed.). **Management for Quality Improvement: The 7 New QC Tools**
ISBN 0-915299-29-1 / 1988 / 324 pages / $59.95 / order code 7QC

Monden, Yasuhiro and Michiharu Sakurai (eds.). **Japanese Management Accounting: A World Class Approach to Profit Management**
ISBN 0-915299-50-X / 1990 / 568 pages / $59.95 / order code JMACT

Nachi-Fujikoshi (ed.). **Training for TPM: A Manufacturing Success Story**
ISBN 0-915299-34-8 / 1990 / 272 pages / $59.95 / order code CTPM

Nakajima, Seiichi. **Introduction to TPM: Total Productive Maintenance**
ISBN 0-915299-23-2 / 1988 / 149 pages / $39.95 / order code ITPM

Nakajima, Seiichi. **TPM Development Program: Implementing Total Productive Maintenance**
ISBN 0-915299-37-2 / 1989 / 428 pages / $85.00 / order code DTPM

Nikkan Kogyo Shimbun, Ltd./Factory Magazine (ed.). **Poka-yoke: Improving Product Quality by Preventing Defects**
ISBN 0-915299-31-3 / 1989 / 288 pages / $59.95 / order code IPOKA

Ohno, Taiichi. **Toyota Production System: Beyond Large-Scale Production**
ISBN 0-915299-14-3 / 1988 / 162 pages / $39.95 / order code OTPS

Productivity Press, Inc., Dept. BK, P.O. Box 3007, Cambridge, MA 02140 1-800-274-9911

Ohno, Taiichi. **Workplace Management**
ISBN 0-915299-19-4 / 1988 / 165 pages / $34.95 / order code WPM

Ohno, Taiichi and Setsuo Mito. **Just-In-Time for Today and Tomorrow**
ISBN 0-915299-20-8 / 1988 / 208 pages / $34.95 / order code OMJIT

Perigord, Michel. **Achieving Total Quality Management: A Program for Action**
ISBN 0-915299-60-7 / 1991 / 384 pages / $45.00 / order code ACHTQM

Psarouthakis, John. **Better Makes Us Best**
ISBN 0-915299-56-9 / 1989 / 112 pages / $16.95 / order code BMUB

Robinson, Alan. **Continuous Improvement in Operations: A Systematic Approach to Waste Reduction**
ISBN 0-915299-51-8 / 1991 / 416 pages / $34.95 / order code ROB2-C

Robson, Ross (ed.). **The Quality and Productivity Equation: American Corporate Strategies for the 1990s**
ISBN 0-915299-71-2 / 1990 / 558 pages / $29.95 / order code QPE

Shetty, Y.K and Vernon M. Buehler (eds.). **Competing Through Productivity and Quality**
ISBN 0-915299-43-7 / 1989 / 576 pages / $39.95 / order code COMP

Shingo, Shigeo. **Non-Stock Production: The Shingo System for Continuous Improvement**
ISBN 0-915299-30-5 / 1988 / 480 pages / $75.00 / order code NON

Shingo, Shigeo. **A Revolution In Manufacturing: The SMED System**, Translated by Andrew P. Dillon
ISBN 0-915299-03-8 / 1985 / 383 pages / $70.00 / order code SMED

Shingo, Shigeo. **The Sayings of Shigeo Shingo: Key Strategies for Plant Improvement**, Translated by Andrew P. Dillon
ISBN 0-915299-15-1 / 1987 / 208 pages / $39.95 / order code SAY

Shingo, Shigeo. **A Study of the Toyota Production System from an Industrial Engineering Viewpoint** (rev.)
ISBN 0-915299-17-8 / 1989 / 293 pages / $39.95 / order code STREV

Shingo, Shigeo. **Zero Quality Control: Source Inspection and the Poka-yoke System**,Translated by Andrew P. Dillon
ISBN 0-915299-07-0 / 1986 / 328 pages / $70.00 / order code ZQC

Shinohara, Isao (ed.). **New Production System: JIT Crossing Industry Boundaries**
ISBN 0-915299-21-6 / 1988 / 224 pages / $34.95 / order code NPS

Sugiyama, Tomo. **The Improvement Book: Creating the Problem-Free Workplace**
ISBN 0-915299-47-X / 1989 / 236 pages / $49.95 / order code IB

Suzue, Toshio and Akira Kohdate. **Variety Reduction Program (VRP): A Production Strategy for Product Diversification**
ISBN 0-915299-32-1 / 1990 / 164 pages / $59.95 / order code VRP

Tateisi, Kazuma. **The Eternal Venture Spirit: An Executive's Practical Philosophy**
ISBN 0-915299-55-0 / 1989 / 208 pages/ $19.95 / order code EVS

Yasuda, Yuzo. **40 Years, 20 Million Ideas: The Toyota Suggestion System**
ISBN 0-915299-74-7 / 1991 / 210 pages / $39.95 / order code 4020

Productivity Press, Inc., Dept. BK, P.O. Box 3007, Cambridge, MA 02140 1-800-274-9911

Audio-Visual Programs

Japan Management Association. **Total Productive Maintenance: Maximizing Productivity and Quality**
ISBN 0-915299-46-1 / 167 slides / 1989 / $749.00 / order code STPM
ISBN 0-915299-49-6 / 2 videos / 1989 / $749.00 / order code VTPM

Shingo, Shigeo. **The SMED System**, Translated by Andrew P. Dillon
ISBN 0-915299-11-9 / 181 slides / 1986 / $749.00 / order code S5
ISBN 0-915299-27-5 / 2 videos / 1987 / $749.00 / order code V5

Shingo, Shigeo. **The Poka-yoke System**, Translated by Andrew P. Dillon
ISBN 0-915299-13-5 / 235 slides / 1987 / $749.00 / order code S6
ISBN 0-915299-28-3 / 2 videos / 1987 / $749.00 / order code V6

Returns of AV programs willl be accepted for incorrect or damaged shipments only.

TO ORDER: Write, phone, or fax Productivity Press, Dept. BK, P.O. Box 3007, Cambridge, MA 02140, phone 1-800-274-9911, fax 617-864-6286. Send check or charge to your credit card (American Express, Visa, MasterCard accepted).

U.S. ORDERS: Add $5 shipping for first book, $2 each additional for UPS surface delivery. CT residents add 8% and MA residents 5% sales tax. For each AV program that you order, add $5 for programs with 1 or 2 tapes, and $12 for programs with 3 or more tapes.

INTERNATIONAL ORDERS: Write, phone, or fax for quote and indicate shipping method desired. Pre-payment in U.S. dollars must accompany your order (checks must be drawn on U.S. banks). When quote is returned with payment, your order will be shipped promptly by the method requested.

NOTE: Prices subject to change without notice.